WISHING WELL

I0139598

Jon Klein

BROADWAY PLAY PUBLISHING INC
224 E 62nd St, NY, NY 10065
www.broadwayplaypub.com
info@broadwayplaypub.com

WISHING WELL
© Copyright 2006 by Jon Klein

First printing: June 2006
I S B N: 0-88145-306-4

Book design: Marie Donovan
Word processing: Microsoft Word
Typographic controls: Ventura Publisher
Typeface: Palatino
Printed and bound in the U S A

WISHING WELL was first produced by The Victory
Theater Center (Tom Ormeny, Maria Gobetti, Robert
E Alschuler and Susan Alschuler, Producers) in Los
Angeles, opening on 11 September 2003. The cast and
creative contributors were:

CALLIE QUAYLE .... Kathleen Bailey
MRS CAUTHEN .... Judy Jean Berns
RICHARD SMALLS .... Tai Bennett
CINDY CAUTHEN .... Tracey Stone
DENNIS QUAYLE .... Joe O'Connor
NEWS ANCHOR VOICE .... Nicolle White Robledo

Director .... Maria Gobetti
Set design .... Gary Randall
Costume design .... Dawn DeWitt
Sound design .... Steve Braverman
Lighting design .... Tom Ormeny

CHARACTERS & SETTING

CALLIE QUAYLE, *thirty-nine*
MRS CAUTHEN, CALLIE'*s mother, sixties*
RICHARD SMALLS, *a neighbor, twenty-three,*
  African-American
CINDY CAUTHEN, CALLIE'*s sister, nineteen*
DENNIS QUAYLE, CALLIE'*s husband, forty-two*

A Victorian home on Bald Head Island, North Carolina.
Summer.

SCENES

ACT ONE

Scene One: Friday afternoon
Scene Two: Friday evening
Scene Three: Saturday morning

ACT TWO

Scene Three: Continued
Scene Four: Saturday evening
Scene Five: Sunday afternoon

for Maria

ACT ONE

Epilogue

(*Preset:* MRS CAUTHEN's *house, lit brightly by the mid-afternoon sun.*)

(*This is a wooden Victorian with a large wrap-around porch, presented on an angle so we view the corner of the house.*)

(*The exterior wall of the house cuts away to show an old-fashioned sitting room, with a library of books and pristine furniture. Steps lead up to the front porch, which contains a swing and outdoor furniture. But the exterior seems a bit neglected, the shrubbery needing pruning and the house paint noticeably peeling. On the side of the house stands an old wishing well, which needs new paint and stone repair.*)

(*After the house dims, the stage lights begin to dim too. Halfway through, there is an enormous clap of thunder, and a sudden blackout on stage.*)

(*As there is a softer rumbling, the aftereffect of the thundercrack, we see a flashlight beam—controlled by* CALLIE—*shining on her own face as she faces the audience.*)

(CALLIE *is thirty-nine. Her manner is somewhat world-weary, with a gently dry wit.*)

CALLIE: As you can see—or as, obviously, you can't see—the power is out. A storm is coming. Some people call this an act of God. The faithful, of course. And the insurance companies. Who put their faith in actuarial

tables. But they believe in God too. God gives them
something to sell. Namely, insurance against the
mercurial whims of the Almighty. Because if God
decides to send a lightning bolt into your bedroom, or
feels like diverting a local tributary into your basement,
there's nothing you can do to stop it. Except maybe
prayer, if you think that might work. But either way,
you can get some money back. *(She moves closer to the
audience.)* That's where I come in. I'm a claims adjuster.
Or, to be more precise, a Catastrophe Specialist. My
firm downplays the religious implications. But they
exist between the lines. See, if God has it in for us, then
the sensible thing to do is to protect yourself against
Him. And insure yourself against those few occasions
when he decides to "act". That's the whole reasoning
for catastrophic insurance coverage. Institutionalized
existentialism. You won't find many Christian Scientists
in the insurance industry. *(She sits on the lip of the stage.)*
Don't get me wrong. I love my job. Determining the
probability of events. That's a pretty cool way to play
God. If you're so inclined. And I usually am. Sure, it's
a game—but name a better one. Risk? Life? Mousetrap?
No, for the sheer entertainment value, nothing beats
playing God. Although there is a bit of a downside.
Which would be...oh, I suppose all the exposure to
extreme human suffering. But I do have a generous
401K plan. I wonder if God does.

(The thunder rumbles again, louder.)

CALLIE: Anyway, this act of God has just left us in the
dark. Literally. So here I wait, outside my mother's
house, near the ocean. And God is hovering around
up there, deciding whether to simply take our power—
or blow us to kingdom come.

(More thunder, getting closer.)

CALLIE: Unless, of course, God is dead. Or too
distracted by events in the Middle East to care about

what happens on a tiny island off the coast of North Carolina. In which case, this is no act of God. I did it myself. Two days ago. With the wishing well. *(She shines the light on the wishing well, then turns off the beam.)*

Scene One

(Two days earlier—Friday)

(Lights slowly come up on the house, again on a beautiful sunny summer day.)

(Two suitcases, one small and one large, are seen on the front porch. But no one is there.)

(CALLIE's mother, MRS CAUTHEN, comes out the front door and sees the suitcases. She is an energetic, if somewhat ill-tempered, woman in her sixties. She looks around.)

MRS CAUTHEN: Callie? *(She walks to the edge of the porch and looks around the yard. She shouts louder.)* Callie! I know you're here! *(She waits for a response, but hears none.)* For a grown woman, you are such a child. *(She heads for the front door, pausing at the sight of the suitcases with disgust.)* How many bags do you need for a weekend? Dollars to donuts you brought more than one pair of shoes. *(She leaves the bags on the porch and goes back in the house.)*

(CALLIE sticks her head out from behind the back of the house. She slinks along the exterior wall and peeks up on the porch. Not seeing anyone, she relaxes. She turns and looks at the wishing well with a challenge.)

CALLIE: Hey. Remember me? *(She holds up a shiny new quarter.)* I'm back. *(She walks to the well and looks inside.)* Pew. Nothing like stagnant water to spoil nostalgia. *(She holds the quarter over the well.)* All right. You know the drill. I wish for something, and you make damn sure it never happens. Ready? *(She closes her eyes to make her wish.)*

(MRS CAUTHEN comes out, then notices CALLIE at the well. She watches, not interrupting.)

(CALLIE throws the quarter in, waiting for the splash. She opens her eyes.)

CALLIE: Spend it wisely. I'll expect your complete indifference, as usual.

MRS CAUTHEN: This is sad.

(CALLIE looks up to the porch. She shows no embarrassment.)

CALLIE: Hello, Mother.

MRS CAUTHEN: You're too old to make wishes.

CALLIE: More of a bribe, really. Hush money.

MRS CAUTHEN: Oh, that's right. You and your sister used to concoct some twisted game.

CALLIE: Nothing twisted about it. It's very pragmatic.

MRS CAUTHEN: Refresh my memory. What's the point of it again?

CALLIE: The point—to use the word of a non-believer—is to make a wish that should be prevented at all costs.

MRS CAUTHEN: And the well prevents it.

CALLIE: Yep.

MRS CAUTHEN: What's the point of wishing for something you don't want anyway?

CALLIE: I didn't say I don't want it. It might be something I want desperately. But it would be wrong to want it. Perhaps even evil.

MRS CAUTHEN: You are so perverse.

CALLIE: Thank you.

MRS CAUTHEN: That wasn't a compliment.

CALLIE: I know. I was being perverse.

MRS CAUTHEN: So what kind of wish was this?
Something horrible, I suppose.

CALLIE: Shameful. Wicked.

MRS CAUTHEN: What makes you so sure the well will
prevent it?

CALLIE: It's working so far.

MRS CAUTHEN: How do you know?

CALLIE: You're still breathing.

(Pause. MRS CAUTHEN squints at her daughter.)

MRS CAUTHEN: I'm too old to carry your bags.

CALLIE: I didn't ask you to.

MRS CAUTHEN: Then get them off the porch. I don't
want the neighbors to get ideas.

CALLIE: What ideas? That you might have a visitor?
Or that you prefer nylon to leather?

MRS CAUTHEN: I didn't ask you here to fight, Callie.

CALLIE: Then I'm at a loss. Who are you and what have
you done with my mother?

MRS CAUTHEN: Don't mess with me, girl. I know you're
my daughter, but I won't take it from you.

CALLIE: Fine. I'm willing to sell.

*(MRS CAUTHEN goes in the house, slamming the screen door
behind her.)*

(CALLIE sits on the porch swing, trying to calm down.)

CALLIE: CALLIE: Less than a minute. That set a new
record.

(A shout is heard from offstage.)

RICHARD: Hello? Miss Cauthen?

(CALLIE *turns to see* RICHARD *enter, and stand at the foot of the porch stairs. He is a handsome African-American man, twenty-three, dressed in tight jeans and work shirt, a bit stained with perspiration.*)

CALLIE: Yes?

RICHARD: You're her daughter, right? Cassie? Carrie?

CALLIE: Can I help you?

RICHARD: You don't remember me, do you? My name's Richard Smalls. I live next door.

CALLIE: Oh?

RICHARD: My daddy ran the junk shop.

CALLIE: My God. Little Ricky?

RICHARD: Oh. Yeah. That's what your mom called me.

CALLIE: You've...grown. You've really grown.

RICHARD: I haven't heard anyone call me that in fifteen years. The "Little" part, anyway. Your Mom still calls me "Ricky."

CALLIE: I'm trying to remember. How did she come up with—

RICHARD: She was a big fan of *I Love Lucy.*

CALLIE: Ah yes. The peak of her ethnic awareness.

RICHARD: Yes, Ma'am.

CALLIE: Oh, Christ. How matronly. I'm not old enough to be a "Ma'am."

RICHARD: Yes, Ma'am. Sorry.

CALLIE: Make you a deal. You don't "Ma'am" me, and I won't "Ricky" you.

RICHARD: Sorry. My upbringing, you know.

CALLIE: Wanna trade?

RICHARD: Umm...

CALLIE: Just kidding. *(She gestures to a porch chair.)* Come on up and have a seat.

RICHARD: Oh, I don't know 'bout that. Your mom...

CALLIE: What about her?

RICHARD: She doesn't care for dirty shoes on her porch.

CALLIE: You're not ten years old any more, Richard. Despite what my mother may think.

(RICHARD pauses, then climbs the stairs to take a chair.)

RICHARD: Well then ... thank you. Thank you very much.

CALLIE: My name's Callie, by the way.

RICHARD: Callie. That's right. *(He indicates her baggage.)* I've seen you come by. Over the years. And your sister.

CALLIE: Ah, yes, Cindy. She'll be here soon.

RICHARD: Special occasion?

CALLIE: I don't really know. Some sort of family meeting.

RICHARD: Been a long time since I've seen the three of you together.

CALLIE: We try to avoid personal contact. The friction causes brushfires. Next thing you know, the National Guard's directing traffic away from the flames.

RICHARD: I see.

CALLIE: Speaking of disaster areas—is it my imagination, or do things look nicer on your side of the fence?

RICHARD: Pardon?

CALLIE: Looks like your father really cleaned things up.

RICHARD: Oh, thanks. That was me, actually. I inherited the business when Dad retired. He's in Boca Raton.

CALLIE: What did you do with all those old rusty cars?

RICHARD: Sold them. To a junkyard.

CALLIE: I thought you were a junkyard.

RICHARD: It's more of a salvage operation now.

CALLIE: Salvage. Meaning you...

RICHARD: Find stuff.

CALLIE: Oh.

RICHARD: Sunken boats, house fires, you name it. Lots of people lose things in an emergency.

CALLIE: Hey. Do you realize we overlap? I do catastrophic insurance.

RICHARD: Hm.

CALLIE: Interesting. Don't you think?

RICHARD: It's just my job. Bring it up, pull it out, brush it off. Whatever it is.

CALLIE: Sounds like a good job.

RICHARD: I do all right. To tell you the truth, I've got other interests.

CALLIE: Ah, a Renaissance man. What other irons do you have on the fire?

RICHARD: My artwork. *(Pause)* I'm an artist.

CALLIE: I heard you the first time.

RICHARD: And you look like I just farted. I didn't, did I?

CALLIE: I'm just trying to suppress my initial response.

RICHARD: Which is what?

CALLIE: Disappointment.

RICHARD: Oh.

CALLIE: It's not you, Richard. I deal with a lot of people who call themselves artists. And I have to compensate them for their art when it gets destroyed. There's nothing worse than trying to put a market value on artwork that might be priceless to its creator— but in reality is worth twenty to thirty-five dollars.

RICHARD: According to who?

CALLIE: Oh, there are formulas for that.

RICHARD: For the value of art?

CALLIE: For the value of anything.

RICHARD: Wow. I had no idea.

CALLIE: There's really not much leeway. Whether it's bought, built, painted or constructed. The minimum value can always be calculated.

RICHARD: What about the maximum value?

CALLIE: No such thing, I'm afraid. Remember what Goering said?

RICHARD: Who?

CALLIE: You know. Hitler's Reich Marshal. He said, "Every time I hear someone talk about art, I pull my luger." *(Pause)* Did I just compare myself to a Nazi?

RICHARD: I think so.

CALLIE: I gotta watch that.

RICHARD: Listen, the reason I came over here...

CALLIE: Oh, of course. You want me to appraise your artwork.

RICHARD: That's not what I—

CALLIE: No really, it's okay. I'm no art critic, but I can give you an appraisal for its value if lost by fire of flood. If that's what you want.

RICHARD: You can tell me what my art is worth?

CALLIE: Maybe more than you think.

RICHARD: Closer to thirty-five than twenty?

CALLIE: Come on, I'd enjoy seeing it. Seriously.

RICHARD: Look, I came over here to tell you something.

CALLIE: Yes?

RICHARD: It's about your mom.

(Pause)

CALLIE: Go on.

(A squealing of tires is heard as a car pulls up in front of the house. They look off.)

RICHARD: I guess that's your sister.

CALLIE: You look relieved.

RICHARD: We should talk another time.

CALLIE: Sure. I'm here two days.

(MRS CAUTHEN comes out of the house with anticipation.)

MRS CAUTHEN: Is that Cindy?

CALLIE: Yes, mother. The apple of your eye just pulled up. Don't restrain your enthusiasm on my count.

RICHARD: That is one nice Vette.

(MRS CAUTHEN turns at the unexpected voice.)

MRS CAUTHEN: Oh. Hello, Ricky.

RICHARD: Mrs Cauthen.

CALLIE: His name's Richard, mother.

MRS CAUTHEN: I know his name, Callie.

CALLIE: But you said—

MRS CAUTHEN: You know, Ricky, it might be a good idea for you to take your shoes off before walking on the porch.

CALLIE: Mother!

MRS CAUTHEN: Just in case. You never know.

CALLIE: You never know what?

RICHARD: Yes, ma'am. Your daughter looks like she could use some help with those bags. *(He quickly moves off the porch, and offstage.)*

CALLIE: Christ, Mother. Can't you be a little more subtle with your racism?

MRS CAUTHEN: It has nothing to do with his color. I'm talking about the soles of his shoes. You have no idea what he could be tracking over here from that junkyard.

CALLIE: Like what? Agent Orange? Plutonium?

MRS CAUTHEN: Maybe. Could be anything from the looks of that place.

CALLIE: All you can see from here is a shed and a wooden fence.

MRS CAUTHEN: That's my point. What's he trying to hide?

(RICHARD returns with two large suitcases, followed by CINDY, dressed for the beach in a halter top and short skirt, wide-brimmed hat and sunglasses, with a handbag.)

(CINDY is nineteen, and compared to the others, has a noticeably pronounced Southern accent.)

(CINDY follows RICHARD at a distance, checking out his posterior with admiration.)

CINDY: Lookee what I found. The last survivin' gentleman on Bald Head Island.

MRS CAUTHEN: Ricky lives next door.

CINDY: I know Richard, Momma. I was livin' right here till two years ago. But this strappin' young feller would hardly ever come by. Why was that, Richard?

(RICHARD *notices* MRS CAUTHEN's *stern gaze.*)

RICHARD: No reason. (*He puts the bags up on the porch without stepping on the steps.*)

CINDY: Well, don't be such a stranger while Callie and I are visitin'.

MRS CAUTHEN: There won't be a lot of time for outside socializing.

(CINDY *gives her mother a hug.*)

CINDY: Oh, hush, Momma. You know I wouldn't let my flirtin' get in the way of my big ol' whoppin' love for you.

(*She gives her mother a noisy kiss.* MRS CAUTHEN *is embarrassed, but pleased.*)

MRS CAUTHEN: Oh, stop it now.

(CALLIE *puts her hand to her throat.*)

CALLIE: Whoa.

MRS CAUTHEN: What's wrong with you?

(CALLIE *holds her hand to her throat.*)

CALLIE: Gag reflex.

MRS CAUTHEN: Let's get these bags inside. I made some lemonade and Chex mix. (*She struggles to lift* CINDY's *heavy bags, and pulls them into the house.*)

(CALLIE *is appalled.*)

CALLIE: Mother, stop that!

CINDY: Don't bang the little one, Momma. C D player.

MRS CAUTHEN: I've got it. *(She disappears inside.)*

(CINDY turns to RICHARD.)

CINDY: So, Richard. You seein' anybody?

CALLIE: Jesus, Cindy.

CINDY: What? Just a little neighborly chat.

RICHARD: I've been a little busy with the yard.

CINDY: The yard? What, you mow lawns?

CALLIE: He has his own salvage business.

RICHARD: Speaking of which. You might consider putting some plywood up.

CALLIE: Plywood?

RICHARD: On the windows. Storm's coming in.

CALLIE: I think I would have heard something about that. My husband's the meteorologist for Channel Three in Wilmington.

RICHARD: Channel three. That would be ...

CALLIE: Dennis Quayle.

RICHARD: The "Cautious Weatherman"?

CALLIE: That's the one.

(RICHARD looks at CINDY, who shrugs with a smirk. He looks back at CALLIE.)

RICHARD: I've got some extra. Just give me a call.

CINDY: Same goes for you.

RICHARD: You ladies have a good time.

CINDY: Can't speak for my sister. But I certainly intend to.

(RICHARD hesitates, turning to CALLIE.)

RICHARD: Maybe I'll take you up on that offer.

CINDY: What offer was that, sis?

RICHARD: To show her some of my artwork.

CALLIE: That would be fine.

CINDY: You can show us anything you like.

(CALLIE *points to something off.*)

CALLIE: Wow. Did you see that thing go?

(They turn and look.)

CINDY: What?

CALLIE: Your libido. Running away from you.

(CINDY *smiles and turns to* RICHARD.)

CINDY: Ain't my sister a caution. I swear, she's nearly as funny as she thinks she is.

RICHARD: Ladies. *(He exits.)*

CALLIE: I think he just insulted my husband.

CINDY: Never mind that. How dare you call me a slut in front of the neighbors?

CALLIE: I said no such thing.

CINDY: I'm just a friendly sort.

CALLIE: You were staring at his ass.

CINDY: Not...by itself.

CALLIE: Good Lord.

CINDY: Well, you gotta admit, those are the sweetest buns outside a French bakery.

CALLIE: I was trying not to look.

CINDY: Why not? You're only human.

CALLIE: That's a poor excuse.

CINDY: Maybe. But it's the best we got. *(She looks at the wishing well.)* Have you tried the well yet?

CALLIE: Yep. Threw in a quarter.

CINDY: A quarter? Used to be a nickel.

CALLIE: I figured—inflation.

CINDY: What did you wish for?

CALLIE: That this entire house, with Momma in it, would rise up and blow away like that scene in *The Wizard of Oz.*

CINDY: That's terrible.

CALLIE: I thought so too.

(CINDY *opens her purse and walks down the stairs toward the well.)*

CINDY: I'll try to come up with something worse. *(She stops on the way there.)* Cal. You wished for a tornado? Or was it a windstorm?

CALLIE: I wasn't specific.

CINDY: Remember what Richard just said? About a storm comin'?

CALLIE: You're thinking...what, the wish?

CINDY: It's a weird coincidence, ain't it?

CALLIE: Nonsense. I just insured ourselves against it.

(CINDY *looks at* CALLIE *seriously.)*

CALLIE: Besides, Dennis would have called. If anything was brewing. They've got radar and storm-tracking instruments up and down the coastline.

CINDY: I guess.

CALLIE: What's a junkman got to predict the weather? A broken barometer?

CINDY: Okay.

CALLIE: Besides, like I said, I made sure it would never happen. With the wishing well.

(CINDY *pulls out a quarter and walks over to the well. She recoils from the smell.*)

CINDY: Holy shit. Smells like a dead animal.

CALLIE: I know.

CINDY: Let's see... (*She holds the coin over the well, trying to keep some distance from the odor.*) I wish someone would break my heart. (*She drops the coin, satisfied.*) Like *that* could ever happen.

CALLIE: What kind of wish was that?

CINDY: Just lookin' for a little romance.

CALLIE: On Bald Head Island?

CINDY: Oh, this place ain't without its prospects. (*She peers over into the next lot.*)

CALLIE: He's not interested, Cindy. And Mother would have a stroke.

CINDY: How would you know who'd be interested? You ain't flirted with a guy since you married "Mister Cautious."

CALLIE: Don't call him that.

CINDY: And as for Momma, her bark is worse than her bite. She's just a big ol' pushover.

CALLIE: I don't think so. I've tried pushing her over.

CINDY: What's she want with us, anyway?

CALLIE: I was hoping you might know.

CINDY: Nope. Just got the call to show up this weekend.

CALLIE: She called your dorm room?

CINDY: Yep.

CALLIE: See, the reason I ask, is I tried calling your dorm room too. At midnight. And your roommate told me she hadn't seen you in weeks.

CINDY: Right...I was staying at the sorority house.

CALLIE: Ah. So you're in a sorority now.

CINDY: That's right.

CALLIE: Which one?

CINDY: Delta...Delta... *(Thinking)* Pi.

CALLIE: Delta Delta Pi.

CINDY: That's right.

CALLIE: Not familiar with that one.

CINDY: Well, you know... It's a new one.

CALLIE: A new charter?

CINDY: Just getting off the ground.

CALLIE: I see. So when Momma called you at your dorm room—

CINDY: My machine. She left a message on my answering machine. Because, you know, I don't sleep there any more.

CALLIE: You sleep in the sorority house.

CINDY: Right.

CALLIE: Funny your roommate didn't mention that.

CINDY: Well, course not. She's the reason I moved.

CALLIE: To Delta Delta Pi.

CINDY: That's right.

CALLIE: Where, I suppose, you have no phone number.

CINDY: What, my own phone? I'm just a sophomore. I ain't made of money, you know.

CALLIE: But enough to buy a Corvette.

CINDY: What, that beat up ol' thing? They practically gave it to me.

CALLIE: "They" being—

CINDY: The owner. A girl in my class.

CALLIE: You said "they".

CINDY: I meant her.

CALLIE: Your roommate said this was exam week.

CINDY: I was exempt. Look, what is this? Twenty questions?

CALLIE: I don't think I'm quite up to twenty.

CINDY: You got somethin' to say, why don't you just say it.

CALLIE: All right. I don't think you're in school at all. I think you dropped out. And you haven't even told our mother.

(Pause)

CINDY: I believe there are refreshments inside. You're welcome to join us. *(She goes into the house.)*

(CALLIE shakes her head. She looks at the audience.)

CALLIE: See that? I haven't stepped foot on this porch in two years. Yet she's the long lost daughter, who gets lemonade and Chex mix. After nine months of school, or pretending she's in school, or whatever the hell she's doing. She's got Mother wrapped so tight around her finger that she can hardly breathe. Someday that old woman's heart will break from the weight of all that devotion. Then Cindy will have to find someone else to make her lemonade. *(She stands up, and walks down off the porch.)* Do I sound jealous? Good. Because my sister is living proof that life, with all its uncertainties, is

predictably, dependably, undeniably...unfair. I mean,
just look at her. I know you have. That's all people
do when she's around. I might as well be part of
the wallpaper. That's what I feel like, anyway.
The wallpaper in this house. Yellow, crinkly,
and peeling away.

(MRS CAUTHEN *calls from inside the house.*)

MRS CAUTHEN: *(Offstage)* Callie? What are you doing
out there?

(CALLIE *yells back.*)

CALLIE: I'm rolling naked on the lawn, Mother.

MRS CAUTHEN: *(Offstage)* Don't track that dirt on the
porch.

(CALLIE *returns to the audience.*)

CALLIE: The real mystery is, what was Mother thinking?
Having a baby so late in life? You've met her. It's hard
enough to imagine her having sex even once. Then she
tries it again nineteen years later? What was that about?
No wonder Dad died soon after. The shock must have
killed him.

(CINDY *is heard laughing from inside.*)

CALLIE: Just listen to her. I wouldn't mind it so much,
except she's so fucking...*happy.* Twenty years old.
With no discernible skill or talent, other than a kind of
natural charm that propels grown men to grovel at her
feet. And women to ignore her callous indifference to
the feelings of others. Natural charm? I call it unnatural.
I'd like to kill her, except she's obviously a witch, and it
would only make her stronger. *(She stands, looks at her
bags, and picks them up.)*

*(The sound of wind as she shivers from the sudden breeze.
She turns to look at the skies, peering for any sign of activity.)*

CALLIE: There's no place like home. *(She carries the bags into the house.)*

(Lights fade.)

Scene Two

(Lights up)

(Later that evening. The lights are on in the sitting room next to the porch, as MRS CAUTHEN, CALLIE *and* CINDY *gather and sit. There is a silver tea set on one of the small tables, and* MRS CAUTHEN *begins to pour a cup.)*

CALLIE: I don't want any, Mother.

MRS CAUTHEN: Yes you do.

CALLIE: No, I really don't. It keeps me up at night.

MRS CAUTHEN: Take it.

(She holds out the teacup to CALLIE. *Slight pause, then* CALLIE *takes it.)*

CALLIE: Oh, for God's sake. At least let me pour the rest.

*(*MRS CAUTHEN *relinquishes the tea over to* CALLIE, *who pours cups for her mother and* CINDY. MRS CAUTHEN *sits down and looks at her daughters.)*

MRS CAUTHEN: I have some rather...unusual news.

CINDY: What is it, Momma?

MRS CAUTHEN: It's about your father. *(Pause)* He's dead.

(Long pause. CALLIE *and* CINDY *look at each other.)*

CALLIE: Well, that is news. You know, rumor also has it that someone walked on the moon.

MRS CAUTHEN: Quiet, dear. This is a serious matter.

CALLIE: Mother, unless senility has completely taken over, you might remember that we all received that news nineteen years ago.

CINDY: I'm not sure I got the news. I was just a baby.

CALLIE: Someone told you eventually.

CINDY: I guess so.

CALLIE: *(Turning to her mother)* So unless you have some new information about his death—

MRS CAUTHEN: I do.

(Pause)

CALLIE: Like what?

MRS CAUTHEN: The date.

(Pause)

CALLIE: The date...of what?

MRS CAUTHEN: His death.

(CALLIE and CINDY look at each other again.)

MRS CAUTHEN: I was a little off.

CALLIE: *How* off?

MRS CAUTHEN: About nineteen years.

(MRS CAUTHEN stands up and goes to the bookshelf. She removes a book, opens it, and pulls out an envelope. She brings it over to CALLIE.)

MRS CAUTHEN: Here. Read it.

(CALLIE is hesitant to take it.)

CALLIE: What is this, Mother?

MRS CAUTHEN: Just read it. It's addressed to you.

CALLIE: How strange. Somebody already opened it.

(MRS CAUTHEN takes a sip of tea.)

(CALLIE *eyes her mother suspiciously, takes the envelope and opens it.*)

CALLIE: There's a letter...and two checks. For...me and Cindy. Two...very large checks.

CINDY: How much?

MRS CAUTHEN: Never mind that now. Read the letter.

CALLIE: "Dear Callie— The doctor give me some bad news. My heart is not too good. So I'm arranging things. I got some money for you and Cindy. I did okay for myself here in Skagway. I weren't too good with the King Crabs, but once I started to charter Salmon runs things picked up." (*She looks at her mother, confused.*) Mother, what—

MRS CAUTHEN: Keep reading.

(CALLIE *returns to the letter.*)

CALLIE: "I'm sorry I didn't see you two grow up, but you can ask your mama about that. Speaking of which, Katie, if you opened this letter and you think you can keep it from my daughters, you better know I got a lawyer who'll call them one week after my death. It does you no good to hide things no more. You got the house, which is more than fair."

(*She looks up at her mother again.*)

MRS CAUTHEN: Keep reading.

CALLIE: "Anyways, this money is all I got, from my savings and the charter boat. Won't do me no good now, so I sold it. But I want you and Cindy to know that you are both my daughters, and nothing will ever change that. I wish you well. Pop." (*Long pause. She lays the letter and checks down on a table, staring at them.*)

(CINDY *picks up the checks. She whistles.*)

CINDY: Callie—these checks are over twelve thousand each.

CALLIE: I know.

(They both turn their gaze from the letter and contents to their mother, who takes a sip of tea.)

MRS CAUTHEN: Well, that's done. See you in the morning.

(She stands up. CALLIE grabs her arm.)

CALLIE: Where do you think you're going?

MRS CAUTHEN: Take your hand off me, child. I don't remember giving you permission to touch me.

CALLIE: You told us he was dead.

MRS CAUTHEN: He is dead. You'll get the calls in a few days.

CALLIE: You lied to us.

MRS CAUTHEN: I did no such thing. Like I said, I just...jumped the gun.

(CALLIE releases her mother's arm in astonishment.)

CALLIE: That's all you have to say about this? You "jumped the gun"?

MRS CAUTHEN: I don't hear Cindy complaining.

CALLIE: Cindy was less than a year old! She didn't even know him!

MRS CAUTHEN: Believe me, it's better that way. Try to be a little more like your sister.

CINDY: Momma—I think Callie's right. You're gonna have to cough up a little more info.

MRS CAUTHEN: Why should I?

CALLIE: He said to ask you.

MRS CAUTHEN: We don't have to do what he says.
He's dead.

CINDY: Momma, please. We're just trying to
understand. We were his kids, you know.

MRS CAUTHEN: *(Sharply)* Of course I know. You don't
have to tell me. *(She catches herself, and takes a seat.)*
All right. What do you want to ask me?

CALLIE: When did he die?

MRS CAUTHEN: Last Monday. In a Fairbanks hospital.
See? I'm telling you more than you even asked.
I'm being very forthcoming.

CALLIE: What happened the first time?

MRS CAUTHEN: What time is that?

CALLIE: Don't be coy, Mother. What happened nineteen
years ago?

MRS CAUTHEN: Oh. Well...the truth is...your father and I
were...having problems.

CALLIE: What kind of problems?

MRS CAUTHEN: That's entirely out of your jurisdiction.

CALLIE: Jesus.

CINDY: Please, Momma. Just try.

MRS CAUTHEN: We were having problems...and he
agreed to go away.

CALLIE: "Go away"?

MRS CAUTHEN: Yes, it was a mutual decision. For all
concerned.

(CALLIE turns to her sister.)

CALLIE: Does this make any sense to you?

CINDY: Where did he go, Momma?

MRS CAUTHEN: Like he told you. Skagway, Alaska. Where he bought a fishing boat.

CALLIE: I distinctly remember a memorial service. I was called home from my first year at U N C. I took the whole semester off.

MRS CAUTHEN: Yes, you were devastated. I was quite sorry to see you go through all that.

CALLIE: You were?

MRS CAUTHEN: Yes, it was very unfortunate.

CALLIE: Then why didn't you offer to help, by, oh, let's see, maybe...telling me he wasn't dead!

MRS CAUTHEN: I thought about it.

CALLIE: But you overcame the temptation.

MRS CAUTHEN: That's right.

CALLIE: Tell me, Mother. When was it that you lost your soul? Or did you ever have one?

MRS CAUTHEN: Insulting me does not accomplish anything.

CALLIE: Are you even human?

MRS CAUTHEN: What do you mean?

CALLIE: See, a real human wouldn't answer that way.

CINDY: Callie—

CALLIE: Have you been listening to any of this? She's pretending she had no complicity in this. (*Turning to her mother*) You do know what complicity means?

MRS CAUTHEN: I do my crosswords.

CINDY: Momma, I'm a little confused. I thought Daddy was lost at sea. Didn't they find his boat in the ocean?

MRS CAUTHEN: His excursion boat, yes. But his body was never recovered.

CALLIE: Jesus. Nineteen years of thinking his lungs filled with salt water. So...let me understand this. He arranged his own disappearance?

MRS CAUTHEN: Certainly not. I did.

CALLIE: What?

MRS CAUTHEN: Do try to keep up, dear. He had already gone to Alaska. He had been gone several days. So I decided that he should die. It would look better.

CALLIE: To who?

MRS CAUTHEN: To whom.

CALLIE: To fucking whomever! What the hell were you thinking?

MRS CAUTHEN: I'm not going to tell you if you use that kind of language.

CALLIE: You ain't heard nothing yet.

CINDY: Let her talk, Cal.

MRS CAUTHEN: Well, like I was saying, it didn't look too good. In those days, a single mother didn't get much respect, especially in a small town filled with fishermen's wives. It felt...demeaning. So I decided that your father should drown.

CALLIE: Am I really hearing this? Or am I experiencing some virus-induced hallucination?

MRS CAUTHEN: Oh, quit acting up, Callie. That kind of hysterical behavior always makes you lose your credibility.

CALLIE: *My* credibility?

CINDY: I still don't understand, Momma. I thought they found the boat.

MRS CAUTHEN: Ah yes, the boat. Well, the truth is, I hired Little Ricky's father to take it out and sink it.

CALLIE: Oh...my God.

MRS CAUTHEN: I considered putting a little suicide note in the cabin. But then I thought how that would reflect on me.

CALLIE: Of course you did.

MRS CAUTHEN: Plus I would have lost all the insurance benefits.

CALLIE: The benefits!

MRS CAUTHEN: Yes, they came in handy.

CALLIE: Mother, do you understand you committed fraud? A criminal act? You could do jail time for this! And now that I've heard all this, so could I! As an accomplice! Christ, Mother! I work for the same insurance company that handled your claim!

MRS CAUTHEN: Hmm. You know, you're right. It might be best if you didn't tell them.

CINDY: Good idea.

CALLIE: *(To* CINDY*)* How can you take this so calmly? We're talking about nineteen years of lies and deceit.

CINDY: Well, that's on the one hand. But this other hand's holdin' a check for twelve thousand dollars.

CALLIE: Don't you resent the fact that she kept you from knowing who your own father was?

CINDY: You know, that *is* rather annoying, Momma.

CALLIE: *Annoying?*

CINDY: Well, like I said, I was just a baby. I can see why you'd be upset, though. Momma, you owe Callie an apology.

MRS CAUTHEN: All right. I'm very sorry.

CALLIE: You want me to forgive you? Are you insane?
I always knew you were bitter and malicious, but
I never dreamed you were evil incarnate. You're a
monster on a mythical scale. You're something that
needs to be slain before occupying a throne.

MRS CAUTHEN: *(To* CINDY*)* I don't think she's accepting
my apology.

CALLIE: Help me, God.

MRS CAUTHEN: I just don't understand, Callie. You lost
me.

CALLIE: No, Mother. You lost me. Nineteen years ago.
When you had my father killed. *(She turns to* CINDY.*)*
Give me a cigarette.

CINDY: You don't smoke.

CALLIE: That's right. I gave it up. About, oh, nineteen
years ago.

(CINDY *reaches into her purse and pulls out a pack.*
CALLIE *grabs it and pulls out a couple of cigarettes,*
throws the pack down and leaves the room. She goes
out on the porch, slamming the front door behind her.)

MRS CAUTHEN: I didn't have him killed.

CINDY: It feels that way to her.

MRS CAUTHEN: I had a good reason.

CINDY: Like what?

(Pause)

MRS CAUTHEN: I can't tell you.

CINDY: I'm very disappointed in you, Momma.

MRS CAUTHEN: Cindy—you and I always got along.

CINDY: Maybe it was easier for you and me, Momma.
It was always just the two of us. I didn't have a memory
to deal with.

MRS CAUTHEN: So now you hate me too?

CINDY: Neither of us hate you, Momma.

MRS CAUTHEN: She does.

CINDY: No she don't. She just thinks she does.

MRS CAUTHEN: It feels the same.

CINDY: I guess so.

MRS CAUTHEN: He was not a good man, Cindy.
You didn't miss much.

CINDY: You know, Momma, the more I think about it—
I would have liked to figure that out myself.

(MRS CAUTHEN *peers at* CALLIE *through the window.*
CALLIE *paces and smokes.*)

MRS CAUTHEN: She shouldn't smoke.

CINDY: That's right. But you can't control everything
people do.

(MRS CAUTHEN *is stung by this.*)

MRS CAUTHEN: I'm tired. Make sure you lock up.

CINDY: Yes, Momma.

MRS CAUTHEN: Don't forget. Everything gets...
locked up. (*She leaves the room. She hesitates, almost
going to the porch, then turns into the house and exits.*)

(CINDY *notices this, then goes outside onto the porch.*)

(CALLIE *peers into the distance, from a corner of the porch.*)

CINDY: You doin' okay?

CALLIE: Didn't we use to see the ocean from here?

CINDY *stands by her sister.*

CINDY: Think you're right. In between those two houses. Now there's a Holiday Inn.

CALLIE: I thought so.

CINDY: As though anyone would take a holiday there. Ain't no beach to speak of, just a tidebreaker full o' sharp rocks. You'd cut your feet open.

CALLIE: The place we grew up.

CINDY: Yep.

CALLIE: Dad kept his boat over there. For the tourists. What few we had.

CINDY: So they tell me.

CALLIE: On his days off—and he had a lot of days off—he used to take me out for a cruise. Total waste of fuel, and Mother complained about it, but he did it anyway. Sometimes he took me up the intercoastal all the way to Wilmington. Other days, out to sea. Strapped me to the chair and told me how to reel in the big ones. Course he stood right behind me. Grabbing the pole whenever I hooked something. Caught a couple of swordfish, a sea turtle, even a marlin. He couldn't believe that one, said it was hundreds of miles off its natural habitat. Know what he told me? "Callie," he said, "I do believe life will never pass you by. Because you can make anything come to you." (Pause. She goes to a porch chair and sits.) I guess Dad was the one that got away.

CINDY: It ain't your fault, Cal.

CALLIE: No shit. You think I'll ever forgive that woman? She took half my life and sent it packing to Alaska.

CINDY: She feels bad too.

CALLIE: Oh, sure.

CINDY: She does.

CALLIE: Well, good. I hope she does. I wish I could make her feel worse. I wish... *(She gets an idea, and stands up.)* ...I wish! *(She looks in the window of the sitting room.)* Where's your purse? Still in there?

CINDY: Don't smoke any more, Cal. That don't help anything.

CALLIE: I don't want a cigarette.

CINDY: Then what—

(CALLIE goes into the house, and digs into CINDY's purse. CINDY speaks to her through the window.)

CINDY: What are you doin'?

(CALLIE finds a quarter, and holds it up triumphantly.)

CINDY: Oh, Jesus. Don't do this, Cal.

(CALLIE comes back out onto the porch.)

CALLIE: Something must be done.

CINDY: Don't kid around, Cal. I got a bad feelin' 'bout this. You wished for a storm, and Richard says there's one out there, just waitin'.

CALLIE: What's your point?

CINDY: What if...the wishes are startin' to come true?

(Pause)

CALLIE: Then you'll have nothing to worry about.

(She heads for the wishing well, CINDY right behind her.)

CINDY: Cal—don't!

(CALLIE holds the quarter over the well.)

CALLIE: I wish Mother would live forever.

(She drops the quarter. They listen to it splash.)

CINDY: That was a horrible thing to do.

CALLIE: Not according to your theory. I just bestowed eternal life.

CINDY: That's not what you wished for and you know it.

CALLIE: Apparently, my dear sister, it doesn't matter what I wish for. And it never has.

CINDY: You have no right to be cruel.

CALLIE: And you don't have the right to assume what I'm feeling. Because you never even had a father.

CINDY: That's not true.

CALLIE: It might as well be.

(CINDY *hesitates, then goes in the house. She starts down the hall, then turns back into the sitting room and retrieves her purse, then grabs her check. She angrily holds it up to the window, to show* CALLIE *before she leaves the room. She turns off the light in the sitting room and disappears into the back of the house.* CALLIE *sits in one of the porch chairs. She begins to cry.)*

(Lights fade.)

Scene Three

(Lights up)

(Saturday morning)

(CALLIE *is asleep in the same chair, covered by a thick quilt.* RICHARD *is gently prodding her awake, holding a thermos. A large, misshapen piece of wood sits on the porch.)*

RICHARD: Miss Cauthen? Hello?

(CALLIE *slowly awakens, blinking at the strangeness of her surroundings, and* RICHARD. RICHARD *pours her a cup from the thermos.)*

CALLIE: Good morning. I guess.

RICHARD: You shouldn't sleep outside. Even in the summer. *(He offers her the cup.)* Here. Hot cocoa.

(She takes it and smells the aroma.)

CALLIE: This takes me back. Ovaltine?

RICHARD: That's right. You remember well.

CALLIE: I remember too well. *(She looks at the quilt.)* Thanks for the blanket too.

RICHARD: Not mine. I expect someone in there brought it out for you.

CALLIE: In there? *(She looks at the house curiously.)*

RICHARD: I know you've got a nice warm bed inside. You grew up in this house.

CALLIE: My mother always kept it a little cold. *(She staggers to her feet.)* Christ, listen to those joints. Sounds like the Fourth of July. *(She notices the wood on the floor.)* What's this doing here?

RICHARD: I brought it for you.

CALLIE: My mother sealed up the fireplace twenty years ago. She had a notion that bats would fly down into the house. Attracted to her scent, no doubt. Thanks anyway.

RICHARD: It's not firewood, Miss Cauthen.

CALLIE: Callie.

RICHARD: Sorry.

CALLIE: I'm feeling old enough this morning without you treating me with respect.

RICHARD: Yes, ma'am—

(She shoots him a look.)

RICHARD: Callie.

CALLIE: So if it isn't firewood, then what...oh.

RICHARD: That's right.

CALLIE: Your artwork.

RICHARD: It's driftwood—from the beach. Well, from the rocks, anyway. Not much of a beach. I go down there and salvage for myself. Coins, shells, crates— and a lot of driftwood. This island is like a great big catcher's mitt.

CALLIE: Very enterprising.

RICHARD: So what do you think?

CALLIE: About what?

RICHARD: What it's worth.

CALLIE: Oh. I see. You want me to appraise it.

RICHARD: Sure. You said you're an expert.

CALLIE: Just for the replacement value. I'm not an art critic.

RICHARD: Okay. So it gets burned in a fire. Or lost in a flood. How much would you give me?

CALLIE: Not me personally. The insurance company. Like I said, there are formulas.

RICHARD: Which you would use. To settle the claim.

CALLIE: Well—yes.

RICHARD: So in the end, you set the dollar level.

CALLIE: I guess.

RICHARD: All right then. What do you think it's worth?

CALLIE: I don't know, Richard. It depends. What do you plan to do with it?

RICHARD: What do you mean?

CALLIE: I mean...what are you going to make? A duck? A mailbox? A sailboat?

RICHARD: I don't think you understand. I made that.

CALLIE: I thought you found it.

RICHARD: I found the original. Then I sculpted it into that.

CALLIE: You—sculpted it.

RICHARD: Sure. Don't you see how polished it is?

CALLIE: Well, yes... But I thought the sea did that. The friction of the surf.

RICHARD: The surf? The surf can tear it apart. It's hard to find a good piece.

CALLIE: Okay. But...what is it?

RICHARD: What do you mean?

CALLIE: I'm sorry, Richard. I can't make out what it's supposed to be. An elephant's trunk? A witch's broom? I'm at a loss.

RICHARD: It's not supposed to be anything. It's abstract.

CALLIE: So you make...abstract driftwood sculpture.

RICHARD: That's right. I call this one "Destiny".

CALLIE: I see.

RICHARD: But I don't expect anyone to guess that from just looking.

CALLIE: That's good.

RICHARD: You don't think much of it, do you?

CALLIE: I've just never... Look, Richard. Driftwood is already abstract. It doesn't need your help. People generally use it to make...recognizable shapes. That's a given.

RICHARD: I know that. Don't you think I know that? That's what makes this unique. It's an artistic choice.

CALLIE: Have you had any success with this? Has anyone ever bought a piece from you?

RICHARD: What difference does that make? People get too used to what's familiar. It loses its value.

CALLIE: Wrong. That's what *gives* it value. Because it gives comfort in an uncertain age. And people need a little comfort.

RICHARD: Don't get upset with me.

CALLIE: I'm not upset. I'm just tired of people making things harder than they are. Some abstract piece of timber that represents Destiny is too damn hard. A duck is easy.

RICHARD: It's not that easy.

CALLIE: I don't mean easy to make. Of course it's hard to make. Because it's easy to recognize. That's what makes it worth something.

RICHARD: Okay. I'll make a duck. Just for you.

CALLIE: I don't want a fucking duck. I want my past back.

(*Pause*)

RICHARD: That'll take a big piece.

CALLIE: Sorry. I'm so sorry. I need to take a shower now.

RICHARD: Callie. Wait.

(*She stands up.*)

CALLIE: Please forgive me. It has nothing to do with you.

RICHARD: I need to tell you something. About your mother.

CALLIE: Oh God. That's the one person I don't want to...come to think of it, I have a question for you.

(CINDY *comes out of the house onto the porch, dressed in sunglasses, denim shorts, a halter top tied high, and high heeled sandals. She carries a tiny purse.)*

CINDY: Hi all. I thought I heard your sexy voice out here, Richard.

(CALLIE *doesn't even acknowledge her presence, focused on* RICHARD.)

CALLIE: Did your father ever say anything about sinking a boat?

CINDY: Oh, no, Cal. Can't we move on?

CALLIE: This doesn't concern you. I'm talking to Richard.

RICHARD: I don't understand. Somebody lost a boat?

CALLIE: No. I'm asking if your father ever deliberately towed an excursion boat out into the Atlantic and sank it. Did he ever mention anything?

RICHARD: But that doesn't make any sense. We're in salvage. We find boats. As a matter of fact, he found your father's boat out there.

CALLIE: Oh. He did, did he?

RICHARD: Brought him a lot of business, to tell you the truth. The Coast Guard had their own people out there looking. But it was like my Dad knew just where to look.

CALLIE: You don't say.

RICHARD: Brought that boat right up and towed it into the harbor. The police didn't find much of anything except a big hole where the rudder should have been. Might have torn on the reef. But that boat was nowhere near the reef when it sank.

CALLIE: Did anyone investigate this?

RICHARD: Don't think so. The waves were pretty rough that night. So no one gave it much thought. But my Dad told me your father could have handled most anything.

CALLIE: How do you know all this? You weren't much older than Cindy.

RICHARD: I heard it all when Dad retired. That's when he showed me the boat.

(CALLIE *looks at* CINDY, *and they turn back to* RICHARD.)

RICHARD: What'd I say?

CALLIE: The...the boat?

RICHARD: Yeah. It's right over there. In the salvage yard. Wanna see it?

CALLIE: Let me take a quick shower. I'll be right back. *(She pauses to speak to* CINDY.*)* Thanks for the blanket, by the way.

CINDY: What blanket?

(CALLIE *points to the lawn chair.*)

CALLIE: That one.

CINDY: Not mine.

(CALLIE *hesitates, and goes into the house.*)

(CINDY *sits on the driftwood.*)

CINDY: What you guys been talkin' bout?

RICHARD: Whether art has any meaning.

CINDY: Oh. Sorry. She's kinda depressed.

RICHARD: No, it was interesting.

CINDY: You're so polite. I like that.

RICHARD: I'm glad. Would you mind not sitting there?

CINDY: Where would you like me to sit?

RICHARD: Anywhere but there. I made that.

(She looks down and stands up.)

CINDY: Oh. I thought it was a log. What is it?

RICHARD: It's my artwork.

CINDY: No, really. What is it?

RICHARD: It doesn't matter.

CINDY: Lemme guess. A tree branch. A big snake.

RICHARD: Never mind. It's just something I brought
to show your sister.

CINDY: Did she get it?

RICHARD: No. She didn't get it.

CINDY: See, that's the problem with Callie. No
imagination. Now me, I can imagine all sorts of things.

RICHARD: Like what?

CINDY: Oh, don't be shy. Not with me. You can be real
direct.

RICHARD: Okay.

CINDY: I've dated black guys, you know. At U N C.

RICHARD: Good for you.

CINDY: Never fails to turn heads in Chapel Hill.

RICHARD: Is that why you do it?

CINDY: One reason, I guess. But there are a few others.

RICHARD: When you say "date", you mean—

CINDY: You know what I mean.

RICHARD: I see.

CINDY: Like I said, you can be real direct.

RICHARD: All right. You're not my type.

CINDY: Course I am. Don't be coy.

RICHARD: I'm not. I'm just not interested.

CINDY: And you don't have to play hard to get.

RICHARD: I'm not playing.

CINDY: All right, give me a reason.

RICHARD: I like older women.

CINDY: Bullshit.

RICHARD: I do. I like women who've been around the block a few times. Experience makes them more interesting.

CINDY: You won't find many girls with more experience than me.

RICHARD: I mean life experience.

CINDY: And that's what turns you on?

RICHARD: Believe it or not.

CINDY: I think "not". I think you're scared of me. Because I'm a white girl.

RICHARD: Oh, please. You seriously need to grow up.

CINDY: Is that right?

RICHARD: That's right. Besides...

CINDY: Yes?

RICHARD: Never mind.

(CINDY *comes close to* RICHARD, *playing with the buttons on his shirt.*)

CINDY: I'm listening.

RICHARD: You don't wanna hear it.

CINDY: Oh, you've said plenty already. And I'm still here.

RICHARD: I don't want to hurt your feelings.

CINDY: I doubt that will happen.

RICHARD: Don't. Please.

CINDY: *Say* it.

RICHARD: You're too skinny.

(Pause. CINDY *shoves him away, furious.)*

CINDY: Hey, if you're gay why don't you just say so?

RICHARD: I'm not gay.

CINDY: Oh, sure. Do you know how many men have turned me down to date?

RICHARD: Not many, I guess.

CINDY: Two. And they were both gay. That's the only possible explanation.

RICHARD: Look, I tried to be gentle.

CINDY: Of course. Queer men are always gentle.

RICHARD: Sorry to break your pattern. But I'm not queer. I'm just not interested.

CINDY: You shouldn't judge people on their looks.

RICHARD: Oh really? And would you have thrown yourself at me if I was just some white boy who lived across the street? *(Pause)* Don't talk about looks to me.

(CINDY, hurt, plops down on the driftwood and sits.)

(He picks up the driftwood and walks off the porch.)

RICHARD: Tell your sister I'll be in the yard waiting for her.

CINDY: My God. It's Callie. You're hot for her.

RICHARD: Now you're just being stupid.

CINDY: Oooh. Looks like I pressed a button.

RICHARD: You don't know your sister very well, do you?

CINDY: And you do, I suppose.

RICHARD: She's in a very beautiful stage of her life.

CINDY: What, old?

RICHARD: You really should try to understand her better. She has an interesting mind.

CINDY: And a big ass. That's what you people like, isn't it?

(Pause. RICHARD stares at her, hard.)

RICHARD: "You people"?

CINDY: That's right. What do you call it? Booty.

(He stares at her hard, then leaves.)

CINDY: Jesus, Cindy. *(She holds her hand to her chest.)* What is he to you? He's nothing. Who cares what he thinks? *(She hits her own chest with her fist.)* Stop beating so fast! It's not like he broke your... *(She turns and looks at the well.)* Oh God. It *is* the well.

(CALLIE comes out of the house.)

CALLIE: I'll be back in a minute.

CINDY: Callie. Listen to me. We have to be careful with the well.

CALLIE: What?

CINDY: It's changing the rules.

CALLIE: What do you mean?

CINDY: Richard rejected me.

CALLIE: My God. Cindy Cauthen may not be irresistible. I hear the Four Horsemen approaching.

CINDY: The well followed my instructions. To the letter.

CALLIE: I guess it would never occur to you that he just doesn't like you.

CINDY: There's more to it. He likes you.

CALLIE: Oh, stop it.

CINDY: He told me so. You're the one. He doesn't even notice me with you around.

CALLIE: Jesus. Really? He's so young.

CINDY: See? It has to be the well.

CALLIE: As opposed to my own natural charm, I suppose.

CINDY: You see what I mean.

CALLIE: I see what you mean, all right. I'm a dowdy old frump who couldn't attract flies.

CINDY: I'm not saying that.

CALLIE: And it's so amazing that a nice young man might be more interested in me than you, that the only possible explanation is the supernatural influence of an ancient wishing well.

CINDY: I *am* saying that.

(CALLIE *exits.*)

(CINDY *picks up some rocks and throws them at the well.*)

(MRS CAUTHEN *comes out on the porch.*)

MRS CAUTHEN: Stop that! Have you lost your mind?

CINDY: I hate it. Stupid thing.

MRS CAUTHEN: It's that silly game you and your sister play. Rational people don't put faith in such things.

CINDY: Yeah, well what are we supposed to believe in, Momma?

MRS CAUTHEN: Not you too. I'll go back to my room.

CINDY: You can't avoid Callie all weekend, you know.

MRS CAUTHEN: What are you talking about? She's the one avoiding me.

CINDY: Oh, stop it, Momma. I had to bring breakfast to your room like this was a four star hotel.

MRS CAUTHEN: That's not my fault. She's out of control. Where is she, anyway?

CINDY: Next door with Richard.

MRS CAUTHEN: Hmmph. I know what he wants with her.

CINDY: So do I.

MRS CAUTHEN: He wants her to help him get his hands on this house.

CINDY: What?

MRS CAUTHEN: His father always had his eye on it. Now his son's working his wiles on your sister.

CINDY: That part I agree with. But it's not about the house.

MRS CAUTHEN: You don't know everything that goes on around here.

CINDY: Neither do you. Did you know Callie spent the night out here? She wouldn't even come in the house.

(MRS CAUTHEN *picks up her blanket.*)

MRS CAUTHEN: How would I know that?

CINDY: Just talk to her, will you? I can't take this any more.

MRS CAUTHEN: After what she said to me?

CINDY: Well, you deserved it.

MRS CAUTHEN: Cindy!

CINDY: I've been thinkin' bout it, Momma. And I'm mad at you, too. I needed my Daddy too.

MRS CAUTHEN: You got along fine without him.

CINDY: I been lookin' for love from every boy I meet. And I don't ever find it. Cause the one man who might have loved me got sent away to Alaska.

MRS CAUTHEN: It's not that kind of love.

CINDY: That's right. It's better.

MRS CAUTHEN: Fine. Blame me if you want. Say terrible things like your sister. I don't care any more.

CINDY: Oh, quit it. So Callie said some terrible things. Because she was hurt. She didn't mean any of it. Haven't you ever done anything like that?

MRS CAUTHEN: Never.

CINDY: Well, I have.

MRS CAUTHEN: That's stupid. Childish.

CINDY: Oh, shut up, Mama.

MRS CAUTHEN: Cindy!

CINDY: I mean it. Who made you the Pope of Bald Head Island? I'm sick of it. Sick of you, sick of Callie, sick of that fucking well. And sick of myself. *(She heads off the porch, and heads for next door.)*

MRS CAUTHEN: Where are you going?

CINDY: To apologize!

MRS CAUTHEN: To your sister?

CINDY: To anyone who will listen!

(She's gone. MRS CAUTHEN *begins to tear up, and wipes her eyes with the blanket.)*

MRS CAUTHEN: Sweet Jesus. They're all done with me. Every last one of them. I'm all alone. *(She goes inside.)*

(The sound of a car is heard, turning onto the driveway and rolling up to the house.)

*(*DENNIS QUAYLE, *forty-two, runs up onto the porch, and loudly knocks on the door.)*

DENNIS: Hello? Anybody home? *(He backs off the porch and yells at the upper window.)* HELLO! IS ANYONE HERE?

(A gunshot is heard from the upper story.)

*(*DENNIS *instinctively ducks.)*

(A slight whistle is heard, then a soft explosion. The sky above the house turns red, with streams of sparks falling.)

DENNIS: What is that?

(The voice of MRS CAUTHEN *is heard from an unseen window above the porch.)*

MRS CAUTHEN: A flare gun! Get the hell off my property.

DENNIS: Mrs Cauthen! It's me! Dennis! Callie's husband!

MRS CAUTHEN: Oh. *(Pause)* Sorry.

(Lights out)

END OF ACT ONE

ACT TWO

Scene Three
(continued)

(Lights up on the same moment)

*(*DENNIS *is rubbing the sparks out of his hair, as* MRS CAUTHEN *comes through the porch door, holding the flare gun.)*

MRS CAUTHEN: I get a lot of Jehovah's Witnesses.

DENNIS: I think my hair's on fire.

MRS CAUTHEN: Let me see.

(He sits on the porch steps, and MRS CAUTHEN *examines his scalp. She spits on his head and rubs it in.)*

MRS CAUTHEN: All out now. Don't worry. You were going bald there anyway.

DENNIS: May I see that?

(She hands him the flare gun, which he takes it to the well, dropping it in.)

MRS CAUTHEN: That was unnecessary.

DENNIS: Mrs Cauthen, you can't shoot at anybody who comes to your door.

MRS CAUTHEN: I didn't aim it at you. Next time try using the phone.

DENNIS: I did try. Why didn't you answer?

MRS CAUTHEN: I turned the ringer off. Too many salesmen. Funeral plots, real estate agents—they all want a piece of me before I kick the bucket.

DENNIS: But your answering machine isn't working.

MRS CAUTHEN: I turned it off too. I don't get any calls anyway.

DENNIS: You got a call from me.

MRS CAUTHEN: Really? I don't remember getting that.

DENNIS: You couldn't hear it. Because you turned off the ringer.

MRS CAUTHEN: Then you should have left a message.

DENNIS: I couldn't leave a message.

MRS CAUTHEN: Well, that's hardly my fault, is it? Did you come for dinner?

DENNIS: No. We're doing a segment from the ferry.

MRS CAUTHEN: Bad weather?

DENNIS: Nothing to worry about. Just a little disturbance coming up from Cuba.

MRS CAUTHEN: Disturbance. You mean a storm.

DENNIS: No reason to call it that. It's just a low pressure system. And the water is warm. So conditions are a little unstable. It won't even get close enough to trigger the Doppler radar.

MRS CAUTHEN: You sure about that?

DENNIS: I'm not one to cause panic. I am the "Cautious Weatherman", you know.

MRS CAUTHEN: We all know. From the blizzard of '99.

DENNIS: That wasn't a blizzard. It was a freak snowfall. Hardly any wind. Not one forecaster predicted thirty inches.

MRS CAUTHEN: Yes, dear. But as I recall, at least they predicted snow. You forecast a light frost.

DENNIS: Frost is snow. In a way. No it's not.

MRS CAUTHEN: Of course, I didn't see the end of your forecast. That's when the power lines came down.

DENNIS: It's not fair to be judged by one freak storm.

MRS CAUTHEN: Don't matter to me. If God decides it's my time, so be it.

DENNIS: So I *have* worried you.

MRS CAUTHEN: No you haven't. Why worry about things you can't control?

DENNIS: Very sensible.

MRS CAUTHEN: Like when you married my daughter. I was dead set against it. But what could I do? I accepted the consequences.

DENNIS: As I remember, you offered to pay me money to leave town.

MRS CAUTHEN: The offer still stands. There's a check for twelve thousand dollars in Callie's purse.

DENNIS: Very funny.

MRS CAUTHEN: Look for yourself. It's in the sitting room.

(DENNIS *looks at her strangely, then goes inside and sees the check still sitting on the table. He picks it up and looks at it.)*

(MRS CAUTHEN *sits in a porch chair.)*

(DENNIS *comes back outside.)*

DENNIS: What in God's name?

MRS CAUTHEN: Don't ask.

DENNIS: Her father had an account in Alaska?

MRS CAUTHEN: Don't ask.

DENNIS: But look at the date.

MRS CAUTHEN: I said don't ask. Deposit it, tear it up, it's all the same to me. But I don't want it in my house.

DENNIS: Well, I'm certainly not going to tear up a check for twelve thousand dollars.

(CALLIE *enters, carrying some faded comic books.*)

CALLIE: That check is made out to me, Mother.

MRS CAUTHEN: But you don't want it.

CALLIE: I haven't decided yet.

MRS CAUTHEN: Surely you have a joint account, Dennis. Deposit it, let it clear, then withdraw as much as you want and move to Key Biscayne.

CALLIE: Stop it, Mother.

MRS CAUTHEN: I hear they have a lot of weather down there. Might be a good career move.

CALLIE: If anyone drives Dennis away, it will be me. Not you. Now go away.

MRS CAUTHEN: Very well. You'll know where to find me when you feel like apologizing.

CALLIE: Screw you, mother.

MRS CAUTHEN: That's not a good start. (*She goes inside the house.*)

DENNIS: Where did this come from, Callie?

CALLIE: Don't ask.

DENNIS: Look at the date on it.

CALLIE: Don't ask.

DENNIS: But why Alaska?

CALLIE: I said don't ask.

DENNIS: This is a lot of money, Callie.

CALLIE: Not enough. Not enough to buy me off.

DENNIS: What does that mean?

CALLIE: Nothing. You want it, you can have it.

DENNIS: Don't you want it?

CALLIE: I don't even want to look at it.

DENNIS: Okay. *(He puts the check on the porch table.)* So. How's the visit going?

CALLIE: I'm trying to decide between murder and suicide.

DENNIS: Oh.

CALLIE: Which way do you vote?

DENNIS: Well ... murder, I guess.

CALLIE: Fine. Murder it is.

DENNIS: Unless I'm the victim.

CALLIE: Not yet. I'll start with my immediate family, and work my way over to you.

DENNIS: I hate it when you come here.

CALLIE: Oh, it's not so bad. Nothing a few years of shock treatment can't fix.

DENNIS: I wish I could help.

CALLIE: Try the well.

DENNIS: No thanks. I've heard all the stories.

CALLIE: Then try helping.

DENNIS: I'd rather try the well.

CALLIE: How come, Dennis? Are you afraid?

DENNIS: Not afraid, exactly. Just a little...scared.

CALLIE: Interesting distinction.

DENNIS: I just always seem to make things worse.
I don't want to tempt fate.

CALLIE: What's so bad about tempting fate?
You did it once.

DENNIS: When?

CALLIE: When you married me.

DENNIS: That's not why I did it.

CALLIE: Still—that was a pretty risky move, Dennis.
You even defied my mother—who would make most
men cry.

DENNIS: I think I did cry.

CALLIE: But you managed to do it anyway. You married
me—despite all the odds and obstacles. So why did
you?

DENNIS: Is this a test?

CALLIE: Absolutely.

DENNIS: Damn it.

CALLIE: I'm waiting.

DENNIS: All right. I can do this. I married you
because...I loved you?

CALLIE: And?

DENNIS: And you loved me.

CALLIE: Not bad, Dennis. You get an A-minus.
The minus is for the hesitation.

DENNIS: Do you still?

CALLIE: Still what?

DENNIS: Love me.

CALLIE: Of course. But it's different now.

DENNIS: Well, sure it's different. Everything's different. Stands to reason it would be different. *(Pause)* How is it different?

CALLIE: We've been married sixteen years. It used to be fifteen. Before that it was fourteen. Do you see what I mean?

DENNIS: Does it involve some sort of countdown?

CALLIE: No. It's like...vanilla ice cream. Everyone starts out with vanilla when they're kids. Then they try chocolate. After a few years, the experiments get bolder—strawberry, pistachio, butter pecan. But eventually, you go back to vanilla. Not necessarily because it tastes the best, or is the most interesting flavor. But because it is basic. Comforting. And utterly dependable. That's how things are now. Understand?

DENNIS: Absolutely.

CALLIE: Are you sure?

DENNIS: Not really.

CALLIE: That's all right, Dennis. Baby steps.

(DENNIS checks his watch.)

DENNIS: I better check in with the crew.

CALLIE: What crew?

DENNIS: Oh. Didn't I mention? We're broadcasting from the ferry. Live at five and again at ten.

CALLIE: Wait a minute. If you came down here from Wilmington...so there *is* a storm coming.

DENNIS: I wouldn't call it a storm. Just a minor disturbance. *(He looks at the check.)* You don't think that check will blow away, do you?

CALLIE: Just take it, Dennis. I told you I don't want it.

DENNIS: If you're sure.

CALLIE: I'm sure.

(He pockets the check.)

DENNIS: I'll try to be back for dinner.

CALLIE: Dinner? Did you tell Mother?

DENNIS: No. I would have, but she was trying to pay me to leave town. Seemed like bad timing.

CALLIE: I'll save you a seat.

DENNIS: I'll bring dessert. Maybe some ice cream.
(He pecks her cheek, and leaves.)

(CALLIE turns to the audience.)

CALLIE: I know. Believe me, I know. I always knew what I was in for with Dennis. Look how we met. I was doing a claim on his Honda Civic. Which had been crushed by a fallen tree—after being hit by lightning. Naturally, Dennis had predicted "partly cloudy." It seemed like an good fit. I predict the value of disaster—keeping it to a minimum. And he predicts the extent and frequency—also keeping it to a minimum. It may not be the passionate romance I imagined as a lovesick teenager. Or even Cindy's age. But that's okay. There are ways to take refuge in...the minimum. *(She leafs through the faded comic books.)* Want to see what I found on the boat? Comic books. Just where I remembered leaving them, in the freezer compartment in my Dad's mini-fridge. Just in case the boat sank. Talk about a self-fulfilling prophecy. Of course, not even a mini-fridge is airtight, so the salt water got to them. By now they're so faded I can barely read the titles. *Nancy. Little Lulu. Heidi. Little Orphan Annie.* Hmm. I sense a pattern here. *(She pulls a sheet of paper out from inside one of them. She squints at it.)* What's this? A drawing? A letter? Can't tell. Is that the word "you"? Was I writing "I love you" to my Dad? Maybe he was writing to me. Maybe...maybe nothing. *(She puts it back, and puts the stack down on a table.)* Whatever it means, it's been in a broken freezer for nineteen years. Which didn't keep it safe, or dry, or legible. It meant something then. But not any more. I guess there's no such thing as a "frozen" moment.

(CINDY *enters from the yard, upset.)*

CINDY: Well, thanks for nothing.

CALLIE: I've got plenty to spare.

CINDY: Why couldn't you be a little more helpful with Richard? Instead of just standing there all alluring in your older woman way?

CALLIE: You do know you're turning slightly insane. Mother's genes are making their way into your brain cells.

CINDY: I was trying to tell him something important. But you kept interrupting.

CALLIE: He was showing us our Father's boat. Don't you call that important?

CINDY: What, that rusty old thing? Why would I care about that?

CALLIE: Wow, you're right. We spent nearly twenty minutes not talking about you. Whatever were we thinking?

CINDY: Shut up. It's not like that. I was trying to apologize.

CALLIE: Apologize for what?

CINDY: I said something bad.

CALLIE: How bad?

CINDY: Really bad. I just don't know how to talk to him.

CALLIE: Well, what do you usually say to boys?

CINDY: See, what usually works for me, is to let them do all the talking. Cause they don't really listen anyway, you know?

CALLIE: Yeah, I know.

CINDY: So, if he's cute, I kinda nod and go "uh-huh", or "hmm." Or, if he's a creep, I tell him to eat shit and die.

CALLIE: I guess that covers it.

CINDY: Not this time. Richard actually listens. That's what got me in trouble.

CALLIE: So think first. Then talk.

CINDY: Damn it. I have no experience at this.

CALLIE: Look. Just find out what interests him. Have a conversation. It's not so hard.

CINDY: Easy for you, maybe. He has a thing for you.

CALLIE: He does not have a thing.

CINDY: He listens to all your boring crap, doesn't he? I call that having a thing.

CALLIE: Well...maybe a little...thing.

CINDY: If there's any justice.

CALLIE: Be nice.

CINDY: So how do I get his attention? Start reading Malcolm Ten?

CALLIE: X. It's not a sequel.

CINDY: Whatever.

CALLIE: He wants you to see him as a person, Cindy. Not just a piece of ass. You should relate to that.

CINDY: Well sure, but, you know, that can be nice too.

CALLIE: Not to him. He wants you to like him for what he is on the inside.

CINDY: But that's so much work.

CALLIE: Look, why is this so important to you? It's not like you have the time for a steady relationship with a local boy.

CINDY: Why not? I'm less than an hour away.

CALLIE: How do you figure that?

CINDY: I'm just up the... *(She stops herself.)*

CALLIE: Up the what?

CINDY: Up the highway. To Chapel Hill.

CALLIE: Which is a five hour drive.

CINDY: I'm too tired for gabbin'. I'm going in.

CALLIE: No you're not. You're staying here and telling me where you're living. Because you're certainly not in school. And you haven't been since Christmas.

(Pause)

CINDY: I'm livin' in Wilmington.

CALLIE: Doing what?

CINDY: I've got a job.

CALLIE: Doing what?

CINDY: I'm in the movies.

(Pause)

CALLIE: Doing whom?

CINDY: They're real movies, Callie. They call them features. There's a big studio in Wilmington. That's where they made *King Kong*. You know, the famous one, the one with Jessica Lange.

CALLIE: Are you saying you're an actress?

CINDY: Well, no. I'm an extra. See, there are a lot of movies that have beach scenes.

CALLIE: Beach scenes.

CINDY: Yeah, especially for teens. Say it's prom night, and all the kids have a beach party. That's where I come in. I wear a teeny little swimsuit—usually a thong—and I toss around a ball or a Frisbee or I walk by carryin' a surfboard. They call that background. Usually a little out of focus. While they shoot the scene in front of me. Big business in Wilmington. Course, most of the movies go straight to video. But I get paid just the same.

CALLIE: How the hell did they find you?

CINDY: Oh, I cut class last fall to go to the beach. And these film scouts came along, and asked me if they could take my picture. With a Frisbee.

CALLIE: Cindy. I don't even know where to start. This is so outrageous. Have you given any thought at all to the future?

CINDY: What do you mean?

CALLIE: I mean, what happens when they put you out to pasture? Because you do realize this so-called career has a built-in obsolescence factor.

CINDY: I ain't no obsolescent. I just turned nineteen.

CALLIE: I'm talking about getting old, sis. When your thighs widen and your tits start to sag.

CINDY: I'll think about that later. When I'm your age.

CALLIE: Listen. Using your body is no way to make money. There's a thin line between what you're doing and prostitution.

CINDY: And that line is the Screen Actors Guild.

CALLIE: But these people don't care about you. They just want to use your body to make some money.

CINDY: Oh, they're not that bad. I've made some friends there. I've got this sort of den mother type, Jezzie, who

does hair and makeup. She's taken me under her wing.
Tells me I'm like the daughter she never had. Gives me
pointers.

CALLIE: Like what?

CINDY: Like who to watch out for, who's got the busy
hands, that kind of thing. She's been around a long
time. She knows the business.

CALLIE: Really? What did she do when she was your
age?

CINDY: Exotic dancing.

CALLIE: Jesus, Cindy.

CINDY: She's really beautiful. And she's older than you.

CALLIE: So there's hope for me too.

CINDY: Absolutely.

CALLIE: Look, if you're so proud of all this, why haven't
you told our mother?

CINDY: I will. I'm just waiting for the right time.

CALLIE: Like what, her funeral?

CINDY: Okay, you know the reason. I don't want to
disappoint her. She always thought I was so smart.
Why, I don't know. But all that reading. And writing.
I almost got carpet tunnel syndrome.

CALLIE: She's paying for your education, Cindy.
You have to return the money.

CINDY: I can't.

CALLIE: Why not? Where's this semester's tuition?

CINDY: In the driveway.

CALLIE: I reiterate—Jesus, Cindy.

CINDY: I'll pay her back. I'm makin' good money.
I've got a cheap little efficiency in Wilmington, and I'm

savin' ten percent of every paycheck. She'll get it all back.

CALLIE: She'll be dead by then.

CINDY: Well, not much I can do 'bout that, is there?

CALLIE: Cindy. You've got to tell her.

CINDY: I will. When I've got the money.

CALLIE: You've got the money. You just got it from our father.

CINDY: Oh. Right.

CALLIE: Tell her.

CALLIE: I can't.

CALLIE: But I can, you know. Think about it.

CINDY: That would be just like you. Fucking up my life just because you're jealous.

CALLIE: Jealous? Of you? Don't make me laugh.

CINDY: You've always been jealous. I'm the one with the boyfriends, I'm the one with the bod, I'm the one that Momma likes, and I'm the one who's young. Instead of locking myself up with insurance forms and a two-bit weatherman more boring than a goldfish. Just cause you threw your life away at the age of twenty-two don't mean I have to. I'm better than that. And I'm better than you.

CALLIE: You're a spoiled little snot, that's what you are. People have always let you get away with anything. Because you have long legs and nice teeth. But you have the soul of a wharf rat.

CINDY: You're going to tell her, aren't you?

CALLIE: Well, if I wasn't before, I sure plan to now.

CINDY: See? Jealous. Good thing Daddy left early.
Otherwise, he might just have loved me more.
And then you couldn't have his shiny memory
all to yourself. What would you do then?

(Pause. CALLIE goes into the house.)

*(CINDY doesn't move for a while. Then she goes to the
wishing well, and peers in.)*

CINDY: I'm low on cash. Do you take credit?

(RICHARD enters behind her.)

RICHARD: Making a wish?

CINDY: Not yet. Got a quarter?

*(RICHARD digs into his pants pocket and pulls out a coin,
which he hands to her. She holds it over the well.)*

CINDY: I wish everyone would hate me. *(She drops in the
coin.)*

RICHARD: You know, with all due respect, you're really
bad at making wishes.

CINDY: It's a game we play. Callie and me. We wish for
the worst possible thing that could happen. To make
sure it won't.

RICHARD: That has a sort of weird logic, I suppose.

CINDY: Except now the wishes are coming true.

RICHARD: Then that *was* a bad wish.

CINDY: Not really. Because it doesn't change anything.
Everyone does hate me.

(She moves to the porch. RICHARD watches her.)

RICHARD: I don't hate you.

CINDY: Of course you do. After what I said.

RICHARD: Well—

CINDY: Richard—I'm really sorry.

(RICHARD *looks at her.*)

RICHARD: Okay. Thanks.

CINDY: What—that's it?

RICHARD: What do you want me to say?

CINDY: How should I know? I've never done this before.

RICHARD: You've never apologized?

CINDY: Well, sure. But I've never *meant* it.

RICHARD: Wow. I'm flattered.

CINDY: I tried to tell you before. But Callie was there.

RICHARD: I had the feeling. That's why I came over.

CINDY: I'm glad you did.

RICHARD: Me too. Hey, don't worry about it. People say a lot of stuff they don't mean.

CINDY: Even you?

RICHARD: Of course.

CINDY: You didn't mean it when you said I was skinny?

RICHARD: No, I meant that.

CINDY: Oh.

RICHARD: But you have other qualities.

CINDY: Like what?

RICHARD: A bad temper.

CINDY: I thought you meant *good* qualities.

RICHARD: You feel things. Not everyone can do that.

CINDY: Not even my sister?

RICHARD: She has a lot of feelings. But she hides them. You vomit them out.

CINDY: That's attractive.

RICHARD: Not at first. But it gets interesting.

CINDY: To who?

RICHARD: To me.

CINDY: You're not just saying that?

RICHARD: I mean it.

CINDY: Because my biggest fear is there's nothin' goin' on inside of me. I mean, the outside pretty much takes care of itself, and I can coast a while on that. But I want somethin' inside too.

RICHARD: Cindy. In the last twelve hours I've seen you go through pain, lust, rage and insecurity. It's quite a show. Like emotional bulimia.

CINDY: No wonder I feel empty.

RICHARD: You're just a little dehydrated.

CINDY: What do you suggest? Gatorade?

RICHARD: Sort of. *(He kisses her—tenderly.)*

(She kisses him back—hard. He gently pushes her away.)

RICHARD: Hey. No bingeing.

CINDY: Okay.

(She grabs him again and puts him in a liplock. He again pushes her away gently.)

RICHARD: Your mother's here, you know. How would she react?

CINDY: Mama? It would kill her.

RICHARD: And that's okay with you.

CINDY: She had a full life.

(She grabs at him, but RICHARD backs away.)

RICHARD: Haven't you ever heard of playing hard to get?

CINDY: Fuck that. Stand still.

(She chases him around the well.)

RICHARD: Time out.

CINDY: Deal. But you do like me?

RICHARD: Sure. For a skinny girl.

CINDY: I always liked you. I used to go up on the crow's nest and spy on you with my binoculars.

RICHARD: You spied on me?

CINDY: Ever since I was twelve. I could see right into your bedroom window.

RICHARD: I don't like where this is going.

CINDY: You had a really good fantasy life.

RICHARD: You don't mean you watched me...

CINDY: Oh yeah. What a waste.

RICHARD: Oh, God. This is not good.

CINDY: First time I've ever seen a black man blush.

RICHARD: I mean, almost every night...

CINDY: Tell me about it.

RICHARD: I can't even look at you.

CINDY: Why not? I liked it.

RICHARD: Come on.

CINDY: And I liked you.

RICHARD: You never even said a word to me.

CINDY: Well...you know...

RICHARD: Yeah. I know. This ain't Chapel Hill.

CINDY: We were kids then. Now we don't care what people think.

RICHARD: Well, I do.

(MRS CAUTHEN *appears at the window.*)

CINDY: No you don't.

RICHARD: Oh yes I do.

CINDY: Like who?

RICHARD: Like your mother. She's watching us from the window.

(CINDY *quickly backs away and leans against the porch.*)

CINDY: Shit.

RICHARD: Just act normal.

CINDY: That's what I was *doing.*

RICHARD: Oh. Right.

(MRS CAUTHEN *walks into the back of the house, out of sight.*)

CINDY: You know what this means?

RICHARD: What?

CINDY: It means...the wishing well is back to normal. Because I asked for the opposite!

RICHARD: You do know how ridiculous that is, don't you?

CINDY: Don't make fun of the well. It's listening.

RICHARD: Why did you start this well business?

CINDY: Oh, it wasn't me. It was Callie. She was about eight years old. And she had a cat. Named Kitty Klism.

(RICHARD *gives her a questioning look.*)

CINDY: I know. Anyway, one day Kitty disappeared. So Daddy told her to ask the wishing well to make the cat come home. Callie says that caused a big fight between them, since Momma said it was cruel to get the girl's hopes up, and they started yelling. So Callie came to the well, and wished that Kitty was dead. It showed up on the porch the next morning.

RICHARD: You know that's sheer coincidence.

CINDY: Wait, there's more. Callie was so happy that Kitty was back, she went back to the well and wished that Kitty would never run away again.

RICHARD: Oh, let me guess.

CINDY: Yep. Disappeared forever. So Callie got the idea that it gave reverse wishes. And she came up with this game to get around the curse. She taught it to me as soon as I could talk.

RICHARD: Look. It's very simple. If you wish for horrible, impossible things to happen, chances are they won't. It has nothing to do with the well.

CINDY: Are you getting mad at me? Because that means the well changed the rules again.

RICHARD: Please. No more talk about the well.

CINDY: Is Momma still there?

RICHARD: Nope.

CINDY: Good. Let's go make out. Your place?

RICHARD: My place?

CINDY: I'm right behind you. She takes off her sandals and runs off.)

RICHARD: Behind me?

CINDY: (Off) Come on!

(RICHARD runs after her.)

(DENNIS *enters, carrying a paper bag. He watches them run off. He comes up on the porch and knocks.*)

(CALLIE *comes to the window.*)

CALLIE: Dennis? Is something wrong?

DENNIS: No, no. I just had a thought.

(*Pause*)

CALLIE: Yes?

DENNIS: Would you like to hear it?

CALLIE: Probably.

DENNIS: Should I come inside?

CALLIE: No. Bad things happen in here. I'll come out.
(*She comes out on the porch.*)

DENNIS: I had a thought about this check.

CALLIE: What about it?

DENNIS: I think we should do something with it.

CALLIE: You do?

DENNIS: Something big.

CALLIE: Really?

DENNIS: Really big.

CALLIE: Wow. Okay. This could be interesting.

DENNIS: Are you ready?

CALLIE: Yes, Dennis. I'm ready. Pause.

DENNIS: Here goes. We should put this check in
a strong money-market fund, for easy access.
But hopefully, we'll never need to touch it. Here.
It's safer with you.

(*He hands her the check.*)

CALLIE: How very...cautious.

DENNIS: Thanks. *(He gestures to the bag.)* Not only that—but I brought some ice cream. Check it out.

(She opens the bag.)

CALLIE: Vanilla.

DENNIS: What you wanted, right? I didn't misunderstand?

CALLIE: No, Dennis. It's exactly what I expected.

DENNIS: Good. I gotta run to the ferry. See you later. *(He runs off to his car.)*

(CALLIE opens the box lid and licks the top of the ice cream. She puts the top back on and goes inside.)

(Lights fade.)

Scene Four

(Saturday night. Inside the sitting room, illuminated by the lamps like the night before.)

(CALLIE sits calmly at the table, as her mother pours herself a small glass of sherry.)

MRS CAUTHEN: So you've come to your senses.

CALLIE: Mother, if you think I'm here to apologize, you have another thought coming to that demented brain of yours. I'm here to talk about Cindy.

MRS CAUTHEN: Cindy? What could you possibly have to tell me about Cindy?

CALLIE: It just so happens I've learned a little secret about her.

MRS CAUTHEN: If it's a secret then what are you telling me for?

CALLIE: I thought you were interested in her welfare.

MRS CAUTHEN: I am. So leave well enough alone.

CALLIE: Wait a minute. Do you know?

MRS CAUTHEN: I know a lot of things, gal. You wanna help Cindy, tell her to stay away from that boy next door. Next thing you know we'll be stuck with a mulatto.

CALLIE: Jesus. Five minutes with you and David Duke looks like a moderate.

MRS CAUTHEN: That boy's just using her to get his hands on this house.

CALLIE: Mother. I'm afraid you're missing the boat.

MRS CAUTHEN: Is that so?

CALLIE: Truth is, Richard is infatuated with me.

MRS CAUTHEN: Un-huh. And I'm the one missing the boat.

CALLIE: I know it seems a little odd.

MRS CAUTHEN: Especially since they've been at his house since this morning. After swapping spit on the front porch.

CALLIE: What?

MRS CAUTHEN: There ain't much entertainment around here. Mostly, I look out the windows.

CALLIE: But that makes no sense.

MRS CAUTHEN: Ah. But wanting a married white woman, twice his age—now that makes sense.

CALLIE: Go away, Mother.

MRS CAUTHEN: You go away. This is my house, remember?

CALLIE: Fine. I'll leave right after I say goodbye to Cindy.

MRS CAUTHEN: You're in for a long wait. She's got jungle fever.

CALLIE: Don't quote Spike Lee, Mother. It's frightening.

MRS CAUTHEN: I watched it on T V last week. Even Spike Lee knows it can't work.

CALLIE: Please.

MRS CAUTHEN: I'll tell you who could make it work. Sidney Poitier. Now he was a looker.

(CINDY enters, and tries to sneak in the house.)

(CALLIE covers her ears.)

CALLIE: I mean it. Stop it. I'm getting nauseous.

(CINDY makes an inadvertent noise.)

MRS CAUTHEN: Who's that?

CALLIE: Probably the N A A C P.

MRS CAUTHEN: Cindy? Is that you?

(Caught, CINDY answers.)

CINDY: Just me, Momma.

MRS CAUTHEN: Come in here, child. Callie has something to ask you.

CALLIE: No I don't.

(CINDY enters the sitting room.)

MRS CAUTHEN: Sure you do. About that boy across the street. I'm sure Cindy knows the answer.

CALLIE: Never mind that. Cindy has something to tell you.

CINDY: I do?

(CALLIE gives her a hard look.)

CINDY: Okay. Let's sit down, Momma.

MRS CAUTHEN: Sounds serious.

CINDY: That depends. Does she have to be here?

(They both look at CALLIE.)

CALLIE: Oh, all right. Do you still have that portable T V?

MRS CAUTHEN: In the kitchen. Where you takin' it?

CALLIE: Out there. Dennis goes on again at ten.

MRS CAUTHEN: There's a perfectly good set in the living room.

CALLIE: No thanks. I wouldn't want to disturb the inner sanctum. *(She goes down the hall and disappears.)*

MRS CAUTHEN: Is this about that boy?

CINDY: What? No.

MRS CAUTHEN: You're just askin' for trouble, you know.

*(*CALLIE *goes out to the porch, with the portable T V.)*

CINDY: This ain't about Richard. It's about school.

MRS CAUTHEN: Bad grades?

CINDY: No—more like...no grades.

*(*CALLIE *turns on the T V, and the sound blares out.)*

CALLIE: Sorry! *(She turns down the sound, then sits in a chair near the window so she can overhear her mother and* CINDY.)

MRS CAUTHEN: I don't follow.

CINDY: See, the thing is, I sort of...dropped out.

(Pause. CALLIE *expects an outburst—but there is none.)*

MRS CAUTHEN: I see. So, what exactly are your...plans?

CINDY: I've got a job.

MRS CAUTHEN: Doing what?

CINDY: I'm in the entertainment industry.

(CALLIE *coughs.*)

CINDY: I'm an actress.

(CALLIE *coughs again.*)

CINDY: I'm an extra.

(CALLIE *coughs again.*)

CINDY: I'm in a swimsuit, okay? Damn it, Callie, why don't you just come in and tell her yourself?

CALLIE: What's that, Cindy? Can't hear you. I'm watching T V.

MRS CAUTHEN: Never mind her. Is this a good job?

CALLIE: Yes, Ma'am. I make good money and the people are real nice. They use me a lot.

MRS CAUTHEN: Use you?

CALLIE: Hire me. I do posters, too. They call that print modeling.

MRS CAUTHEN: What about my money?

CALLIE: You mean the tuition. Okay. I got that all worked out. I can pay you back with the check Daddy left me.

MRS CAUTHEN: That's his money, not mine. I won't take that.

CALLIE: I guess I could sell my car.

MRS CAUTHEN: No, you need that too. I imagine you gotta have a car to work in the entertainment industry.

CALLIE: It does help.

MRS CAUTHEN: All right then. You just...pay me when you can.

CINDY: So you're not mad or anything?

MRS CAUTHEN: You're a pretty girl, Cindy. You're smart to use what God gave you. As long as it makes you happy.

(CINDY *and her mother hug.* CALLIE *peers into the room in disbelief.*)

CALLIE: What the fuck is going on in there?!!

MRS CAUTHEN: You talk like that in your movies?

CINDY: I usually don't talk at all.

MRS CAUTHEN: Good girl.

(CALLIE *storms into the house and confronts her sister.*)

CALLIE: You won't get away with this. (*She turns to her mother.*) You can't possibly let her get away with this.

MRS CAUTHEN: Be quiet, Callie. This is none of your business.

CALLIE: You let her get away with murder!

CINDY: I don't believe I've murdered anyone recently.

CALLIE: Watch and learn.

MRS CAUTHEN: I'm too tired to fight, Callie. I'm going to bed.

(CINDY *stretches and yawns.*)

CINDY: Me too. I declare, this day has plum worn me out. Night, Momma.

(*She kisses her mother on the cheek.*)

MRS CAUTHEN: Good night, dear.

CINDY: Sweet dreams, Sis.

CALLIE: Fry in Hell, you unholy bitch.

CINDY: Whatever.

(CINDY *exits the room. We hear her climb the stairs and close her bedroom door.*)

MRS CAUTHEN: Be civil, Callie.

CALLIE: Civil? What if I had told you I was leaving
school? And bought a car with tuition money?
You would have hung me out to dry.

MRS CAUTHEN: Probably.

CALLIE: Let me ask you something, Mother. When did
you start to hate me? Did it happen gradually, or was it
something specific?

MRS CAUTHEN: You're taking this all too personally.

CALLIE: I agree. Nothing in this house has anything to
do with me. Least of all you. *(She leaves the room and goes
to the back of the house.)*

MRS CAUTHEN: Callie—

*(MRS CAUTHEN starts toward her, then stops. She goes
outside, preoccupied. She turns up the sound on the T V.)*

(A female NEWS ANCHOR is heard from the set.)

NEWS ANCHOR: *(T V, V O)* —but the kittens are all safe
tonight, and ready for adoption . Now let's head over
to Dennis Qualye, the "Cautious Weatherman." Dennis,
where are you?

DENNIS: *(T V, V O)* Well, Liz, I'm standing on the
Southport ferry, connecting the mainland to Bald
Head Island, a rural community—

MRS CAUTHEN: Rural!

DENNIS: *(T V, V O)* Which at this moment is the closest
point to the storm.

NEWS ANCHOR: *(T V, V O)* So now it's a storm?

DENNIS: *(T V, V O)* Yes, Liz, the National Weather
Service has upgraded the status of that low pressure
system, to a Tropical Storm. They've named it Dorothy.

NEWS ANCHOR: *(T V, V O)* Dorothy? Like in *The Wizard Of Oz?*

DENNIS: *(T V, V O)* Umm...perhaps so, Liz. I'm not really familiar with that reference.

MRS CAUTHEN: Jackass.

NEWS ANCHOR: *(T V, V O)* Are the residents in any danger?

DENNIS: *(T V, V O)* Nothing to worry about. Yet. But we'll keep an eye on any changes.

(A fierce gust of wind suddenly blows. The screen door on the porch bangs open. The sound of broken glass and a car alarm offstage. The noises obscure the television.)

(MRS CAUTHEN scurries into the house to shut the windows in the sitting room. She doesn't hear the rest of the broadcast.)

NEWS ANCHOR: *(T V, V O)* Dennis? Dennis? Are you there? Did we lose our feed... Can anyone... I'm... Hold on... I'm getting... I'm told that a sudden gust of wind swept Dennis over the side of the ferry into... Is he... Is he all right? ...Hello? Anyone? ...We've lost radio contact with the crew. Hopefully Dennis... We'll return to this breaking story when we get more information. We'll be right back.

(The T V goes to a current commercial.)

(MRS CAUTHEN comes back outside, chuckles in recognition at the commercial, then turns off the T V. She unplugs it and takes it into the house, shutting and locking the door behind her.)

(CINDY appears at the back of the house, dressed in a dark, hooded sweatshirt. She slinks along the side of the house, listening. She clutches a small photo album. She sprints behind the wishing well, looks at the house, then runs next door.)

(Lights down)

Scene Five

*(Sunday morning. The sky is beginning to darken.
A few branches have dropped from the trees.)*

*(*DENNIS *walks into the yard. His clothes are dry, but
otherwise ruined—torn, ragged and stained with caked
mud. He is barefoot, except for a pair of cheap flip-flops.
He hesitates below the steps, peering at the upper floors.)*

(A scraping sound is heard from within the wishing well.)

*(*DENNIS *turns, hearing the noise.)*

*(He sees an arm encased in black rubber come out of the well
and grab onto the side.)*

*(*DENNIS *looks for a weapon to defend himself. He sees a large
branch in the yard, and grabs it.)*

*(By now, the figure has made its way out of the well,
and pulls up a wet trash bag. It is in full scuba gear,
including oxygen tank.)*

*(*DENNIS *approaches the figure, holding the branch above
his head.)*

DENNIS: Drop it.

*(The figure drops the bag, then stops him with an upraised
palm. It does a "just a minute" gesture. It digs into the bag,
looking for something.* DENNIS *waits. The figure pulls out
a flare gun.)*

RICHARD: *(Muffled)* You drop it.

DENNIS: I happen to know that's a flare gun.
I put it there myself.

*(*RICHARD *shrugs.)*

DENNIS: It's probably waterlogged.

RICHARD: *(Muffled)* Probably. Feel lucky?

(RICHARD *points the gun at* DENNIS. RICHARD *pulls off his hood and oxygen mask, as* DENNIS *drops the branch. They both yell to the house, simultaneously.)*

DENNIS:	RICHARD:
Call 9-1-1!	Somebody call the police!

(CALLIE *comes out of the house.)*

CALLIE: What's going on?

RICHARD: This derelict just threatened me with a tree branch.

DENNIS: And this wacko just threatened me with a flare gun.

CALLIE: Richard—that's my husband.

RICHARD: What? The weather guy?

DENNIS: My name is Dennis Quayle, thank you.
And stop waving that thing around.

RICHARD: This thing? It's waterlogged. (*He tips it and water comes out of it.)*

CALLIE: What do you call this, Richard? Performance art?

RICHARD: Just exploring the well. I bet no one's been down there in forty years.

CALLIE: I can't imagine why.

DENNIS: What about me? Don't you care where I've been?

CALLIE: If you like. What's with your clothes, Dennis? You smell like a dead fish.

DENNIS: You mean you don't know?

CALLIE: Know what?

DENNIS: It's all over the T V. And the radio.

RICHARD: Oh my God. Is that you? I heard it on the shortwave. But I didn't make the connection.

CALLIE: Heard what?

RICHARD: Well, apparently...I'm dead.

(Pause)

CALLIE: Dead.

DENNIS: Not dead exactly. But missing. And presumed dead.

RICHARD: This is the guy that got swept off the Southport ferry.

DENNIS: There, see?

CALLIE: When did this happen?

RICHARD: Last night. They got the Coast Guard out there looking for him.

CINDY: What did you do? Swim to shore?

DENNIS: I tried, but the undertow was strong. It pulled me out to sea.

CALLIE: My God, Dennis!

DENNIS: When suddenly I bumped up against a big piece of driftwood. I managed to hold on to it, keep afloat, and dogpaddle my way back. Came ashore right next to the Holiday Inn. Too late to call anyone. So I took a room. Used a wet credit card and spent the night there. When I woke up, I turned on the T V and found out I was presumed dead.

*(*CALLIE *hugs her husband.)*

CALLIE: It's like a miracle!

DENNIS: Like these flip-flops? Six ninety-nine in the gift shop.

CALLIE: Pretty good deal.

RICHARD: I thought so.

RICHARD: Back up a second. You were saved by a piece of driftwood?

DENNIS: This is the creepy part. I brought it up to my room—my only luggage, I guess—and I noticed something strange about it, under the lamp. That driftwood had a word on it, carved with a knife. It said...

RICHARD: "Destiny."

(Pause)

DENNIS: That's amazing.

(CALLIE turns to RICHARD.)

CALLIE: You threw it back?

RICHARD: Well, you didn't like it. And I was pretty pissed off. So I dropped it off the fishing pier.

DENNIS: Am I missing something here?

RICHARD: We gotta call the police. They've got Search and Rescue out there. *(He pulls out a cell phone.)*

DENNIS: Wait a minute.

RICHARD: What?

DENNIS: I'd rather you didn't.

RICHARD: What are you talking about?

DENNIS: I sort of...like it. You know...being dead.

(Pause)

CALLIE: Dennis. I won't have all the men in my life pretending they're dead. It makes me look bad.

DENNIS: I'm just saying—let's discuss it.

CALLIE: Let's not. Why don't you put those clothes in the laundry, and take a nice hot shower?

DENNIS: I took a shower at the hotel.

CALLIE: Well, take another one.

DENNIS: What do I wear?

CALLIE: Look in my suitcase. I brought a jogging suit.

DENNIS: But I don't—

CALLIE: Just do it.

DENNIS: All right, all right. But no calls. I'm dead until further notice. *(He goes into the house.)*

RICHARD: Destiny. I knew it was the right name.

CALLIE: Makes sense now.

RICHARD: Look, we have to report this.

CALLIE: It must be shock. Just give him a minute.

(MRS CAUTHEN comes out of the house.)

MRS CAUTHEN: Your husband is in my bathroom.

CALLIE: I know, Mother. Don't have him killed.

MRS CAUTHEN: He smells like dead fish.

CALLIE: He can light a match.

MRS CAUTHEN: You'd have to burn down the house for that smell to go away.

CALLIE: Don't tempt me.

(MRS CAUTHEN turns to RICHARD.)

MRS CAUTHEN: What the hell are you doing in that get-up?

RICHARD: Uh...well...Cindy and I were talking...

(MRS CAUTHEN calls inside the house.)

MRS CAUTHEN: Cindy! Come out here!

(CINDY calls back, from inside.)

CINDY: *(Off)* I'm sleeping!

(MRS CAUTHEN calls back.)

MRS CAUTHEN: Oh, well, in that case—come out here!

CINDY: *(Off)* Just a minute!

MRS CAUTHEN: What's in the bag, Ricky?

RICHARD: Well, Cindy and I were talking...

MRS CAUTHEN: You said that already. Although I don't think "talking" is the word you're looking for.

CALLIE: Leave him alone, Mother.

MRS CAUTHEN: I intend to. After he tells me what's in that bag.

(CINDY comes out barefoot, having thrown on some quick clothes, and carrying sandals. She yawns in exhaustion.)

CINDY: What's going on?

MRS CAUTHEN: It seems your friend Ricky has taken an interest in the well. A deep interest.

CINDY: Oh, it's okay, Momma. I told him he could scoop up the coins.

CALLIE: The coins? Our coins?

CINDY: He offered to split 'em with us.

MRS CAUTHEN: *Split* them? That's my well.

CINDY: Oh, Momma. When were you ever going to empty it? You're lucky he offered his services while you're still on two feet.

MRS CAUTHEN: I don't care if I'm on two feet or six feet under. Nobody touches this house—or anything on this property—without my permission.

CINDY: Jeez.

RICHARD: Want me to put them back?

CALLIE: Maybe you should. Stealing from the well could be bad luck.

RICHARD: If you don't mind a little advice, Miss Cauthen—

(CALLIE *makes a "buzzer" sound.*)

RICHARD: Callie.

(CALLIE *makes a "bell" sound.*)

RICHARD: It may not be my place to say. But I think this well is a bad influence. It might have started as a game. But it's messing with your heads.

CALLIE: Oh, I don't take it seriously.

RICHARD: You say you don't. But you do.

MRS CAUTHEN: I've been telling her that for years.

RICHARD: The thing is—neither of you know how to wish very well.

(*Pause*)

CALLIE: Daddy.

CINDY: What about him?

CALLIE: Remember his last words? "I wish you well."

CINDY: He just didn't know what else to say.

RICHARD: I found something else down there.

(*He brings* CALLIE *to the bag and opens it, showing her the interior.*)

CALLIE: What is it?

(*He removes a large piece of bone from the bag, and places it on the lip of the well.*)

RICHARD: If I'm not mistaken, that's the skull of a cat.

CALLIE: Kitty Klism! The wishing well killed my cat!

RICHARD: It did no such thing. The cat just fell in and died. That's what I'm trying to tell you. It's all coincidence.

CALLIE: No. This well hates me. It always has.

MRS CAUTHEN: That's because it's evil.

CINDY: Mama, please.

MRS CAUTHEN: It's evil, I tell you. It's the hellmouth.

RICHARD: I give up.

CINDY: Let's go to your house. And take off that rubber.

CALLIE: There's a phrase I hope you don't use too often.

CINDY: Very funny.

MRS CAUTHEN: I don't get it.

CINDY: She means—

RICHARD: Cindy!

CINDY: Right. Let's go.

(CALLIE *watches them go, then picks up the cat's skull. She places it on the lip of the wishing well.*)

MRS CAUTHEN: Are you going to make a wish?

CALLIE: I made my last one. Know what it was? That you would live forever.

MRS CAUTHEN: Meaning the opposite, of course.

CALLIE: If you believe in such things.

MRS CAUTHEN: Which you do.

CALLIE: Nope. Right now I don't believe in much of anything.

MRS CAUTHEN: I can't have that, Callie.

CALLIE: Too bad. You don't control everything.

MRS CAUTHEN: No. I don't. But I can give you an explanation.

CALLIE: Nothing to explain. It's a clear and simple fact. You prefer your other daughter.

MRS CAUTHEN: *(Softly)* She's not my daughter.

(Pause. CALLIE stops and turns.)

CALLIE: What are you muttering about?

MRS CAUTHEN: Your father and me—how do I put this? We were lucky to have you. Understand? I guess he managed to get some pleasure from it—but not me. I never did. You think I'd let him touch me like that— at the age of forty?

CALLIE: I try not to think about your sex life.

MRS CAUTHEN: You know how men are. I guess that's why he looked elsewhere.

CALLIE: You mean—for pleasure.

MRS CAUTHEN: No, for sea bass. Do I have to spell it out for you? He got some young girl pregnant.

CALLIE: Oh my God. So...Cindy's not your daughter.

MRS CAUTHEN: That's what I said, isn't it? Lower your voice.

CALLIE: I never knew. I was away at college.

MRS CAUTHEN: Good thing, too. I couldn't leave the house for six months. Pretending.

CALLIE: Nineteen years of my life. Dissolves in a day. Then it all dissolves again—a day later.

MRS CAUTHEN: What else could I do? Leave her in the hands of that young slut? She didn't even want her. I raised her as my own.

CALLIE: So that's why you sent Daddy away.

MRS CAUTHEN: Oh, of course not. He did that on his own. He was in love with her. They went to Alaska together.

CALLIE: He...wanted to leave?

MRS CAUTHEN: Mainly because of you.

CALLIE: Me?

MRS CAUTHEN: He couldn't stand the thought of you finding out the truth. Things were different in those days, you know. He was ashamed. And rightly so. There's no more shame any more. Every time I turn on the talk shows I see these people, talkin' bout their dirty laundry like they're proud of the stains. Don't know if that's any better.

CALLIE: It's better. Believe me, compared to these last two days, that is definitely better.

MRS CAUTHEN: I'm sorry, Callie. I really am.

CALLIE: So it was really his choice. He walked away.

MRS CAUTHEN: He knew you could handle it, Callie. We both did. You're the strong one in this family. We always knew that you'd pull through. And you did.

CALLIE: What are you talking about, Mother? I've been unhappy for the last nineteen years.

MRS CAUTHEN: So there were a few side effects.

CALLIE: Then why do you... You always act like Cindy's your real daughter. Not me.

MRS CAUTHEN: Well, just think about it, girl. Cindy needed extra help from the start. Her father abandoned her. If anyone needed a little extra love, it was her. Not you.

CALLIE: But she grew up spoiled and arrogant. You don't see it.

MRS CAUTHEN: Of course I see it. Always did.
What that girl needed the most was a good whoopin'.
But she'd never get it from me. And she never will.

CALLIE: You gave it to me. Plenty of times.

MRS CAUTHEN: Because you're my daughter. *(Pause)*
Are you going to tell her?

CALLIE: Are you?

MRS CAUTHEN: I don't know.

CALLIE: I think you should.

MRS CAUTHEN: I don't know. What if she wants to find
that awful woman?

CALLIE: You think she could?

MRS CAUTHEN: Who knows. She left your Daddy years
ago. Could have come right back here for all I know.
She was just some stripper from Wilmington.

CALLIE: A stripper. You mean...an exotic dancer?

MRS CAUTHEN: I guess that's what they called them
then. Made them whores sound a little more acceptable.

CALLIE: I really think you better talk to Cindy.

*(CINDY and RICHARD enter, catching them off guard.
RICHARD carries a large object, wrapped in newspaper.
He puts it in front of CALLIE.)*

RICHARD: For you.

CALLIE: What do you mean?

RICHARD: I took your challenge.

CALLIE: What do you call this one? Time? Existence?
Phenomenology?

RICHARD: Just open it.

(CALLIE unwraps the package.)

CALLIE: It's...a mermaid!

CINDY: Not just any mermaid. Can't you tell?

MRS CAUTHEN: My goodness...it's Callie!

CALLIE: Is that really me?

RICHARD: I had Cindy find a picture of you.
Just to show you I could do it if I wanted to.

CALLIE: This is extraordinary work.

RICHARD: What do you think? Closer to twenty or
thirty-five?

MRS CAUTHEN: It's worth whatever's in the bag.
You can keep it.

CINDY: What, all of it?

MRS CAUTHEN: This will go in my sitting room.

CINDY: But Richard said there might be two hundred
dollars down there.

RICHARD: Oh, more than that.

MRS CAUTHEN: That sounds reasonable.

CINDY: But what do I get?

MRS CAUTHEN: The back of my hand if you don't be
quiet.

CINDY: No fair!

MRS CAUTHEN: I bet you're hungry after all that carving.

RICHARD: Now that you mention it—

MRS CAUTHEN: I have a nice big Sunday ham.
Come on in.

RICHARD: In the house?

MRS CAUTHEN: Sure. I might even find a cold beer in
the back of the fridge.

RICHARD: Well then... Okay. Thank you, Ma'am.

MRS CAUTHEN: You're welcome, Ricky.

CALLIE: His name is Richard, Mother.

MRS CAUTHEN: That's what I said. *(She rubs the artwork.)* Just look at it. Guess that explains what you and Cindy were doing all night. *(She turns to him.)* At your house.

(RICHARD freezes.)

RICHARD: Umm...

MRS CAUTHEN: Doesn't it?

RICHARD: Yes. That explains it very nicely.

MRS CAUTHEN: Good. Oh, and Ricky? *(She points to his feet.)* Shoes. *(She goes in the house.)*

CINDY: I'll protect you.

(RICHARD sits on the steps.)

CINDY: I'm starting to like "Ricky". I think it's kind of cute.

(RICHARD takes his shoes off as CINDY goes inside.)

CALLIE: Ah, young love.

RICHARD: Callie—about your mother. I never got the chance to tell you—

CALLIE: Oh, I know what this is about. She won't sell.

RICHARD: What?

CALLIE: She won't sell the house. No matter the price.

RICHARD: I don't want this house.

CALLIE: But your father did, right?

RICHARD: You kidding? My dad turned the dogs on every real estate agent come by here. Wouldn't even let them reach the doorbell.

CALLIE: Oh. Then what—

RICHARD: It happened about a week ago. I was coming down my driveway, and I saw Mrs Cauthen. She was lying on the porch.

CALLIE: Lying? Here?

RICHARD: I think she had a fainting spell. My guess is diabetes. A lot of women her age have trouble with that. I got her some lemonade, and she took to it.

CALLIE: Oh my God. My last wish.

RICHARD: Not again. Do me a favor. Seal up that well once and for all.

CALLIE: Right. You're right. I can make things happen. And I can make things change.

RICHARD: That's right.

CALLIE: I'll get her to a doctor. If I have to tie her up and drag her there behind my car.

RICHARD: Oh, she was pretty scared. I think she'll go without a fight.

CALLIE: Humor me.

RICHARD: Okay. Anyways...thanks for the inspiration.

CALLIE: No, thank you. For making me look so beautiful.

RICHARD: Shoot, that part was easy.

CALLIE: Well, I'm very flattered. Even though I know you don't really mean it.

RICHARD: Of course I mean it.

CALLIE: I mean the way Cindy thought you meant it. At first. She thought you were hot for me.

RICHARD: Oh. No. Sorry. I don't chase pregnant women. But I do think they're beautiful.

(CALLIE *is stunned.*)

CALLIE: How did you know? I haven't told anyone!

RICHARD: In the blood, I guess. Like my Dad finding your father's boat. Things don't hide from us.

CALLIE: From you, maybe. But your Dad had a little help.

RICHARD: What do you mean?

(CINDY *and* MRS CAUTHEN *call from offstage, in unison.*)

CINDY & MRS CAUTHEN: Rickeee!

CALLIE: Never mind. Destiny calls.

RICHARD *resignedly goes inside.*

(CALLIE *pages through the comic books, preoccupied.*)

(DENNIS *comes out, dressed in a pink cotton jogging suit, and strapping on a "fanny pack".*)

DENNIS: I'm not dead anymore.

CALLIE: You sound disappointed.

DENNIS: Well, it's not very practical, is it? And I can't have all those people risking their own lives, looking for me.

CALLIE: What's this all about, Dennis? You really wish you were dead?

DENNIS: No. I just liked...not having to be that guy.

CALLIE: What guy?

DENNIS: The guy I've always been. Cautious. Focused. It felt good to be rid of him. Being dead made me feel—

CALLIE: Alive?

DENNIS: I know it sounds ridiculous.

CALLIE: Maybe you don't want to be dead. Maybe you just need a change.

DENNIS: That's impossible. You know how I feel about change.

CALLIE: You almost drowned, Dennis. Things *have* changed.

DENNIS: You think?

CALLIE: And I think you like it.

DENNIS: I do. God help me, I do. But what if that's it?

CALLIE: There will be some big changes—for both of us. You can count on it.

DENNIS: When?

CALLIE: Let's see how you feel tomorrow. Change may not seem so appealing.

DENNIS: No way. Dennis Quayle may be alive. But the "Cautious Weatherman" stays dead.

(DENNIS grabs her and kisses her.)

CALLIE: You're right. Change *is* good.

(They kiss again.)

(Strong thunder is heard. They both look up. The sky gets darker, and the wind gets stronger, from here to the end of the play.)

CALLIE: I hate ironic weather.

DENNIS: Oh. I forgot to tell you. There's a hurricane coming.

CALLIE: What?

DENNIS: I just checked. The latest readings say we'll be in the left wall of the storm. That's always the weakest wall, but this one may get up to a Category Two. You should take your mom and your sister and evacuate.

(MRS CAUTHEN comes out on the porch in time to hear the last words of DENNIS.)

MRS CAUTHEN: Fat chance of that.

DENNIS: It may not be safe here.

MRS CAUTHEN: It's never been safe here. That's no reason to turn tail.

DENNIS: Then ask that neighbor kid to put up some plywood over the windows.

MRS CAUTHEN: No thank you.

DENNIS: Mrs Cauthen—I know I usually minimize the weather. But not this time. A Category Two hurricane will cause flooding and power outages. Maybe worse.

CALLIE: Go on. I'll handle her.

MRS CAUTHEN: You think I'd take advice from a man in a pink jogging suit? He looks ridiculous.

DENNIS: I do?

MRS CAUTHEN: Yes.

DENNIS: Good. I'll wear it for my report. Dennis Quayle— "The Ridiculous Weatherman." At least it's different.

(He gives CALLIE a passionate kiss.)

(MRS CAUTHEN is a bit startled by this.)

(DENNIS exits.)

MRS CAUTHEN: What was that all about?

CALLIE: He loves me, I suppose.

MRS CAUTHEN: Well, even so, no call for that kind of behavior.

(RICHARD and CINDY come out running. RICHARD pulls on his shoes, while CINDY struggles with a gigantic umbrella.)

CALLIE: Where do you think you're going? Richard says a hurricane's coming.

RICHARD: Fantastic! That's the best time to go beachcombing. I once found a crate full of electric razors.

CINDY: I've never seen a hurricane. In person.

CALLIE: There's a good reason for that!

(Thunder again.)

CINDY: Here comes Dorothy! You and your little dog too!

CALLIE: Richard! Before you go, can you give us some plywood?

MRS CAUTHEN: You'll do no such thing! I don't want that stuff scratching my windows.

CALLIE: Mother, if this thing hits, you're not going to have any windows to scratch.

MRS CAUTHEN: That's all right. When God decides it's my time then he can have me. I'm ready to go.

(RICHARD gives CALLIE a business card.)

RICHARD: Here. Call my cell phone if you change your mind.

(RICHARD, CINDY and DENNIS run off, yelling at each other in a cacophony of voices over the now constant thunder.)

(CINDY stops and turns.)

CINDY: Hey sis! I just heard the news! Congrats!

MRS CAUTHEN: What news is that?

(Thunder obscures CALLIE's reply.)

CALLIE: I'm pregnant!

MRS CAUTHEN: What?

CALLIE: I'm going to have a baby!

MRS CAUTHEN: What kind of baby?

CALLIE: Human, I think!

MRS CAUTHEN: This is just like you—to pull something like this!

CALLIE: Sorry for the inconvenience! I'll keep the placenta off your porch!

MRS CAUTHEN: Give me that phone number. We need some plywood!

(She takes the card and goes into the sitting room, where she picks up the phone and dials the number.)

(In a repeat of the first moment of the play, there is a clap of thunder, a bolt of lightning, and a blackout.)

(The storm abruptly stops, as CALLIE snaps her fingers.)

(CALLIE'S face is illuminated by her flashlight, as in the beginning of the play. She stands on the porch.)

CALLIE: And we're back where we started. With an act of God. The storm—which is just sitting out there, deciding what to do next. *(She comes down to the lip of the stage.)* Will it pass by harmlessly? Or will it live up to its namesake, and blow this house and everyone in it to Oz? Who knows? Not the weathermen. Not the wishing well. And certainly not the insurance company. Which gives me second thoughts about my chosen profession. And about God, too.

(A low rumble from the skies. CALLIE looks up, unafraid.)

CALLIE: Think about it. In the last two days, my father came back to life, then died again. While my husband died and came back to life. My sister isn't exactly my sister, my mother isn't immortal, and my cat never ran away. And I'm going to have a baby, long after I gave up on the idea. Do those seem like the acts of a Supreme Being? If God does exist, He must suffer from Attention Deficit Disorder.

(Another rumble)

CALLIE: I think I'm going to have to quit my job.
Because I no longer believe in catastrophic insurance.
We should be *welcoming* catastrophe into our lives.
Because that's what makes us come alive. *(She picks up
the cat skull.)* Alas, poor Kitty. You knew this well.
(She puts the skull on the rim of the well.) Time to take
Richard's advice and seal this thing up. It's become
irrelevant, along with my career and most religions.
So what else is there to believe in? *(She looks out over
the ocean.)* Love, I suppose. Love and plywood. *(She goes
to the porch.)* Don't know what will happen. But here it
comes.

*(She sits down on the porch, watching the storm come, as the
thunder and wind increase. She smiles.)*

END OF PLAY

9 780881 453065